ISBN 978-1-331-35555-7
PIBN 10178562

This book is a reproduction of an important historical work. Forgotten Books uses
state-of-the-art technology to digitally reconstruct the work, preserving the original format
whilst repairing imperfections present in the aged copy. In rare cases, an imperfection in
the original, such as a blemish or missing page, may be replicated in our edition. We do,
however, repair the vast majority of imperfections successfully; any imperfections that
remain are intentionally left to preserve the state of such historical works.

1 MONTH OF
FREE
READING

at

www.ForgottenBooks.com

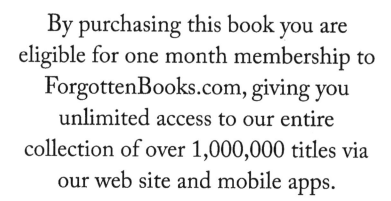

By purchasing this book you are
eligible for one month membership to
ForgottenBooks.com, giving you
unlimited access to our entire
collection of over 1,000,000 titles via
our web site and mobile apps.

To claim your free month visit:

www.forgottenbooks.com/free178562

English
Français
Deutsche
Italiano
Español
Português

www.forgottenbooks.com

Mythology Photography **Fiction**
Fishing Christianity **Art** Cooking
Essays Buddhism Freemasonry
Medicine **Biology** Music **Ancient**
Egypt Evolution Carpentry Physics
Dance Geology **Mathematics** Fitness
Shakespeare **Folklore** Yoga Marketing
Confidence Immortality Biographies
Poetry **Psychology** Witchcraft
Electronics Chemistry History **Law**
Accounting **Philosophy** Anthropology
Alchemy Drama Quantum Mechanics
Atheism Sexual Health **Ancient History**
Entrepreneurship Languages Sport
Paleontology Needlework Islam
Metaphysics Investment Archaeology
Parenting Statistics Criminology
Motivational

TO SAN FRANCISCO AND BACK.

BY

A LONDON PARSON.

Chas. H. Mason
2/15/16

PUBLISHED UNDER THE DIRECTION OF
THE COMMITTEE OF GENERAL LITERATURE AND EDUCATION,
APPOINTED BY THE SOCIETY FOR PROMOTING
CHRISTIAN KNOWLEDGE.

LONDON:
SOCIETY FOR PROMOTING CHRISTIAN KNOWLEDGE;
SOLD AT THE DEPOSITORIES:
77, GREAT QUEEN STREET, LINCOLN'S INN FIELDS;
4, ROYAL EXCHANGE; 48, PICCADILLY;
AND BY ALL BOOKSELLERS.

[Reprinted from the "People's Magazine."]

LONDON·

PRINTED BY JAS. TRUSCOTT AND SON,
Suffolk Lane, City.

CONTENTS.

CONTENTS.

TO SAN FRANCISCO AND BACK.

CHAPTER I.

THE VOYAGE OUT.

THOUGH what forms an agreeable recollection to me revives the memory of wearisome hours to not a few, some of our readers may care to know the impression which an ocean voyage made upon one who had never crossed the Atlantic, or indeed any of the great seas, before. Fortunately for me, I am in one respect a good sailor, and entirely escaped the misery in which the majority of my fellow-passengers passed the first few days of our voyage.

By getting to Liverpool betimes, and immediately going on board the "China" in her tender, which happened to be leaving the landing-stage as I reached it, I secured an early chance of a room to myself—a great luxury, for two berths in a cabin of about eight feet square is close work, especially when shared for some nine or ten days.

B

We went on board on a Saturday, in a small steamer, another carrying the luggage. The mail came out afterwards in a separate tender. We had a perfectly smooth sail to Queenstown, where we were delayed eleven hours for the last mail from London *via* Holyhead. The long ship lay out in Queenstown Harbour, standing as steady as a pier in the flat water, while a fringe of wailing gulls hung round us for scraps, and showed into what clean and graceful shapes even the garbage of a steamboat may be transformed. But we sorely grudged the delay, as it drew heavily upon our chances of fine weather. At last the mail came off in a tender—eighty-four sacks of letters—and, as soon as this vessel was made fast alongside, was run on board by a train of men as fast as they could trot. We began to move while this process was being carried on. Then our pilot stepped on board the small steamer, which left us. We had still one link left to the Old World, in the shape of a shore boat. This clung to us for some time, probably in hopes of picking up a job in the shape of some forgotten message or parcel.

At last the order came from deck, "Let go!" and though those of our readers who are familiar with the passage to America may smile at my sentiment, it was a touching moment when this last home tie was loosened and the boat fell astern, dancing in the foam of our screw.

"Full speed" was now marked by the indicator on deck. Leaving the last lighthouse on the Irish coast, our head was pointed for New York, and our engines throbbed day and night like a great iron heart which sent its pulse through every beam and plank and spar, till it paused to pick up our pilot on the other side of the Atlantic.

Our first experience of the ocean was—so it looked —a boundless midnight plain of molten lead. There was not the faintest whisper of a wind. The red August moon came out and laid a track of gold upon the water, while two bright lines of sapphire light sprang from the ship's bows. We were passing through a highly phosphorescent sea. The sight was most beautiful.

Soon, however, the bright fabric of hope that we should carry this weather with us was rudely dissipated. The " China " is some 320 feet in length, over all. Her upper deck is flush or unbroken for about 300 feet. Next morning, as I stood by the taffrail, this long deck rose like a hill in a straight white road, and then, as we topped the crests of the great moving ranges of water, slid down as if the world were sinking. It was our first experience of the Atlantic " swell." At first we saw no ships. Though on the high road between Europe and America, we passed day after day without seeing a single sail. Of course if the ocean were flat, and vessels made the straightest run from point to point, we should have seen many. The world, however, being round, gives a choice of courses from Liverpool to New York about equal in distance. Some captains always take a southern one, while others, when there is not much ice, go far enough north to sight Cape Race. The loneliness of the ocean is most touching. Morning after morning as I went on deck there was the same round horizon, in which the great waves sometimes showed like islands, and yet not a dot of a sail was to be seen. Mother Carey's chickens kept us company, and now and then a solitary gull visited us in mid-ocean. But our chief external signs of life were whales, of which we saw divers. One morning early I was standing in the ship's bows, looking westward, when a fine fellow heaved his long brown back up, and spouted, apparently not more than eighty yards before us. He seemed so near that I thought I could have thrown a stone upon him. His alarm, however, at seeing the "China" under full steam rushing at him at a rate of some fifteen miles an hour, was excusably great. So he dived faster than he rose, and I have no doubt has made a most exaggerated yarn out of the fright he got among the whales of his society.

On board these fine Cunard ships everything is carried on with the greatest regularity. The meals provided for such passengers as can eat them are numerous and excellent. Breakfast at half-past eight, lunch at twelve, dinner at four, tea at seven, and supper at nine, are a mockery to some, but those who do not suffer find the sea air wonderfully appetising. The ship's company, all told, consisted of 120 men, of whom 30 or 40 were stokers. There are seven engineers, and the captain has four officers and a purser and a surgeon under him. We found these gentlemen very obliging.

I expected to be called upon to say the service on Sundays; but owing to some misunderstanding, a rule had recently, so I was told, been made or followed, that the captain or surgeon should read the service. The crew attended, but as there was no singing, and the noise of the throbbing screw nearly drowned the reader's voice, it was but a dreary act of worship.

The temperature of the air well out on the Atlantic remains nearly the same, about 48° or 50°, summer and winter. "We know no seasons here," said the first officer to me one day; "they are made for the land. Whether I leave New York half frozen, or with the thermometer at 120°, it is all the same. When we get 400 or 500 miles out the mercury stands at about 50°."

The winds are most capricious. They veer about and shift from soft to strong, and back again, continually. The fact is that the sudden changes experienced here often arise not so much from the wind falling or rising as from the ship's passage from one "belt" of weather to another. One morning we would be tearing through the water under sail and steam, with heavy plunging, but a dry deck. Then we would pass into lumpy, windless water, "like a boiling pot," as the mate said, and soon afterwards have to face a head sea which sent waves tumbling in over the ship's bows and rushing along the main deck nearly to the stern. One carried off in its passage great store of the cook's apparatus, and made a sudden wreck of pans and potatoes.

The chief, indeed the ever seriously recognised dangers, arise from fog, during which, in some seasons of the year and in some places, the ship runs the risk of encountering icebergs, especially on the banks of Newfoundland, and, when shore is being reached, ships. But when fog comes, they still drive on "full speed." That brings the ship out of it sooner, and enables it to answer the helm better if occasion should arise. In fog a horrible whistle, if it may be called a whistle, is kept going. But it sounds more like the scream of a mad bull, with a sore throat.

We had experience of this; and there is something awful in the sensation while you stand in the ship's bows, seeing nothing, but rushing onwards with a speed and force that would smash up the whole concern if an iceberg were struck, or make a collision with another vessel horrible.

At last we cleared the fog. When about 400 miles

from port there came dancing up from the horizon a yacht-like schooner with large white sails. This held our pilot. The mainsail of his boat had an enormous black 1 marked upon it. The deciphering of the number of the pilot-boat was a matter of anxiety to twenty-four of our passengers, who had made a sweep-stake of 1*l.* each, and drawn their numbers betimes. Curiously enough two acquaintances of mine, fellow-travellers, had drawn respectively Nos. 1 and 17. The one who drew No. 17 bought an interest in No. 2, to be, as he said, near his friend. The first pilot-boat was No. 1 : it supplied us with a pilot. The next two numbers we saw were 2 and 17. The chances against this coincidence are almost incalculable. However, we got our pilot betimes. He was a little man, in a landsman's dress, with a wide-awake hat, and one small gray eye. As the first who comes is taken, the New-Yorkers push out far for a chance. I was told that the pilot got 150 dollars, or about 30*l.*, for bringing us in.

The first sign of land was the Fire Island Light-house ; then came the low hills of Long Island ; and at about four o'clock on Tuesday, August 31, we steamed into the grand harbour of New York, alive with great white steam ferries, whose engines worked above deck.

The surgeon from the Quarantine, in a white straw hat, boarded us, and brought news that Oxford had

won the boat-race. Every one seemed wholly possessed
and penetrated with this event. The Custom-house
officer began talking about it directly he got on deck;
the driver of the coach to the hotel brimmed with the
subject; and the waiters at supper found time to have
their say upon the matter.

I ought to mention how we mainly spent our time
on board. There were men of divers nations, but
most were Americans. Among the passengers were
a few of some distinction. We had a parcel of eager
Yankee children who incessantly played "sea quoits"
—in which the quoit is a small ring of rope pitched
at a wooden peg, and not counted unless it is a ringer.
And as if the plunging of the ship were not enough,
they must needs have swings. But the quoits and
swings were in no request for the first three or four
days. Many of the passengers played at "shovel-
board." But pleasant conversation with fresh and
agreeable acquaintances was the business of the day.
It must do any man good, if not a settled misanthrope,
to be thus thrown into the company of utter strangers.
He is sure to meet some who look at facts from
another point of view than that to which he is accustomed, and who put forward their opinions with
intelligence. We had a world of talk, and nothing
could make an approach to America more wholesome
than the kindly sentiments of the Americans whom
an Englishman is sure to meet in his voyage to their

country. We English had a good deal of pleasant joking with our cousins at a very peremptory notice stuck up in the ship that we should write our ages, occupation, last legal residence, proposed domicile, &c., on the back of our tickets, by order of the Government of the United States. We told them it reminded us of an entrance into Austria, whereas we thought we had been going to a land of freedom. But the Americans are an eminently law-loving people, and very fond of regulations. In my bedroom at the Fifth Avenue Hotel, I found nailed inside the door not only a card with the usual directions concerning the conduct of the house, but extracts from Acts of Congress respecting the liabilities of innkeepers and hotel-keepers, and sections of an "Act to prevent fraud or fraudulent practices upon or by" them. At the Custom-house, too, we had each to enter in a printed form the number, nature, and contents of our "pieces" of luggage, and sign it before they were examined. All was most orderly and precise. There were, on that occasion at least, no screaming "touters" and hackney-coach drivers. We went quietly enough to our vehicle, and the luggage was put upon its roof by civil attendants of the hotel without any hint of a "tip." The only fuss was a little squeezing from some of the friends of the passengers who wanted to get to them in the Custom-house. I happened to go back for a parcel, and the way in which the officer at the gate said, "Passenger: pass him in," showed the quickness with which those who had just arrived were noticed. At this hotel all went on with the regularity of clockwork. It is an immense establishment, and eminently American. Everything was beautifully clean, and I found the attendants very civil. It holds 1,100 guests, and appears to be quite full. Four of us English arrived there together. When we sat down to dinner, an official came with a request from the managers that we would accept from them a bottle of excellent champagne, as a compliment to us on our arrival. We seemed to be almost the only Englishmen in the hotel.

CHAPTER II.

FIRST WALK ABOUT NEW YORK.

LET me try to give you some of my impressions of New York with the bloom on them. In visiting a new country there are many surface details to which the tourist soon becomes accustomed, but which at first strike him with all the interesting freshness of contrast. I do not pretend to provide statistics of population and commerce, or to furnish grave political intelligence, but simply to say what caught my eye in two days' prowling about New York. I hoped to return to it on my way back from the West, and, using introductions, to see something of its religious and educational institutions. At first I merely prowled, with curiosity alive to those little features of outside life which it presented to one who had just landed in America for the first time, and a pleasant sense of the facility with which the English traveller is able to take in at once by eye and ear foreign impressions made in his own tongue. Thus I simply jot down the impressions which come uppermost as I recal them.

The city struck me as having a Parisian air. The bright sky, the trees in the streets, the abundance of green shutters, the panes of bad glass in many of the shop windows, the roomy white-painted saloons or cafés, the white straw hats with black ribbons worn by many of the men, the large-lettered, many-coloured advertisements and notices, the loose harnessing of the horses, had a French appearance.

The next thing which I found myself noticing was the slowness of the pace at which the vehicles moved. Contrary to my expectation, there was not that strife and bustle which marks the outside of London life. The omnibuses, here called stages, and all painted white, do little more than creep. They have no conductors, and no seats outside. You know the sharpness with which in London you are invited to go to the " Bank " or " Royal Oak," and the peremptory smack, stamp, or ring with which the conductor stops or starts the 'bus. Here the driver makes no sign, but crawls along as if he had no interest in a fare. You hail him, get in behind, pay him through a hole in the roof with a bank-note for 10 cents, or 5d. (the fixed fare for all courses), when you enter the vehicle. Then you rumble and bump over, I should think, the worst paving-stones in the world till you want to alight, giving a signal for the purpose by pulling a bell inside. There are no cabs, but, beside the " stages," a large number of street cars, seating about twenty-five persons inside and none out. These run on tramways in the chief streets, and move somewhat faster than the 'buses. The fares of hackney-coaches, mostly with two horses, are absurdly high, and the drivers are the most extortionate rascals in the world. I did not employ them; but every one, none more than Americans themselves, speaks ill of the race. A Hansom cab company is being established in New York.

The police wear blue cloth sacks, with a metal badge on the breast, and, in summer, wide-brimmed white straw hats. They are all thin, and seem chosen for their inches, which are many.

There are—at least I saw—no street beggars, wandering organ-grinders, or Punches. Everybody seems bent upon an errand, though he does not bustle. I missed at once the tattered men who loaf about London; also the blear-eyed, sodden groups outside public-houses, and the street Arabs.

There is, no doubt, plenty of vice and debauchery in New York, but in strolling by night about its streets I can only say that I did not detect that class which pollutes the great arteries of London. This surprised me, for some of the papers in the hotel reading-room contain many advertisements which a respectable English journal would not publish. But I must say what I saw.

With regard to other street features, I was much

struck with the condition of the upper part of Broadway, which is the chief thoroughfare of the city,
nearly parallel to the Fifth Avenue. This latter is
full of grand, mostly chocolate-coloured and detached,
private residences. In starting from my hotel in the
morning towards the " Central Park "—the Hyde
Park and Kensington Gardens of the place—I walked
up Broadway, which is traversed by numbers of
omnibuses, and in this part by cars. I soon noticed
grass growing in the gutters and between the stones
of the pavement. The patches of this became larger,
till at last I came to three geese, a cow, and a calf,
contentedly grazing in the Oxford Street of this great
city. The houses die down to wretched white-washed
wooden cabins, set anyhow, and inhabited by Irish,
before the most fashionable resort of the citizens is
reached. The park itself—not "central" as yet, though
called such—is admirably laid out with walks, drives,
shrubberies, and ornamental pieces of water ; but the
city is not built up to it. At the other end of Broadway,"down town," every inch of ground seems precious;
but the "West-end," as it were, before you get to the
park, is strikingly incomplete. The New-Yorkers
are, I suppose, too busy to smarten it up till they
want it in earnest. Thus a portion is left to an
irregular settlement of hovels and their poor tenants.
Yet, as I said, the poorest people have all apparently
work to do. Some of the cars are driven by as

uncombed Irish as you may see in the Seven Dials; and when later in the day I crossed the ferry to Jersey City to recover a rather cumbrous article left on board the "China," which lay there, I had to carry it myself through the streets to a parcels' delivery office, that it might be sent to my hotel. Not one of the "poor" people in the streets applied for the job. I saw plenty passing by, but there was not a soul "hanging about." In London, by the wharves, I should have found too many idlers glad to earn a sixpence. Here I could not get a spare hand, though I looked and asked for one.

Everything is dear, as well as labour. Wages are high, but so are prices. I paid at a little shop 5d. for a box of matches I should have given 1d. for in London. A gentleman with me had a "soda and brandy" at the bar of our hotel, for which we found he had to pay 2s. The common necessaries of life are dear, as well as its small luxuries. I am afraid to say what my companion paid for an ordinary chimney-pot hat. Locomotion is cheap, but living is terribly expensive.

The shops are not showy, but large and good when you get inside them. The people in the streets are generally thin—many are tall. The men are better-looking than the women. Few wear full beards, most shaving off all but the moustache.

New York, as our readers know, is an island, with

a population about one-fourth that of London. Parallel avenues traverse it lengthways; these are cut at right angles by streets. The traffic between the city and its suburbs—Jersey City and Brooklyn—is carried on by immense and numerous white ferry-boats, which can take some fifteen or twenty vehicles, horses and all, under cover, besides a large number of foot-passengers, for whom covered accommodation is found in another part of the boat. The fare by them for foot-passengers is 3 cents, or 1½d. Their engines work aboveboard, and they move with as much steadiness as if they were sliding on ice.

Besides these there are many river steamers. Their size and equipment are amazing. Let me try to describe the " St. John," which plies on the Hudson. It is 417 feet long, 80 feet wide, and has three decks. It is larger than the largest ocean Cunard steamship. Its saloons are furnished as sumptuously as any drawing-room, having prints, expensive photographs, stereoscopes, &c., on the tables. It has bedroom accommodation for 600 persons, and will carry, they say, 3,000. One saloon, surrounded with cabins, that I looked into, was about 150 feet long, 20 feet high, and lit with magnificent clustered *gas* chandeliers. The dining-rooms are elaborately provided with everything seen in a first-class hotel. Crowds of civil negroes, in spotless white jackets, wait at the tables, which are ornamented with artificial flowers. There are, of course, extensive kitchens, cellars, and ice-houses. Ornamental fountains or taps of iced water are dispersed through the ship. There are bars where you can order any kind of drink you please, hair-dressers' shops, bookstalls, &c., in these vessels. Large mirrors, soft-piled carpets, the most exquisite cleanliness (even the door of the stoke-hole was of white panel, with white china handles, and quite clean), entirely remove the idea of your being on board a river steamer. Other appliances for comfort and convenience are perfect. The washing apparatus is as good as that in a London club-house. Smoking is strictly prohibited, except in certain portions of the ship. The arrangements for tickets, baggage, &c., are admirable. There is no noise or bustle. I ascended the Hudson to Albany in one of these floating hotels. The pace at which they move through the water is prodigious. With the tide, the one I was in would go twenty-five miles an hour.

I fancy that some of your readers will think I am exaggerating in this account of the New York river boats; but I am not. Americans are justly proud of them; and although I had heard they were excellent, they took me entirely by surprise. The whole of these monster ships are painted white, even to the decks. Altogether the fares are very reasonable. First, second, and third classes are supposed to be unknown here, though in fact on some of the railways there are tickets marked " first class," and if you use a sleeping-car you pay a little more. On board the steamers the poorest people fight shy of the luxurious saloons. But there seemed to be no poor passengers on board the boat I travelled in from New York to Albany. Where, I asked myself, are the ill-dressed, ill-mannered people one might expect to meet where hundreds share the same journey? I looked for them in vain. There is, indeed, one notorious American habit which is recognised on board the steamer by an abundant supply of white china spittoons. Fewer, much fewer, indulged in this habit than I expected. I am bound to say, however, that an American who does spit "whips creation." For inexhaustible fertility of juiciness commend me to an American spitter.

The scenery on the Hudson is very beautiful. Villas and mansions stud its banks. We stopped a few hours at Albany, the metropolis of New York State. Here was the same bad pavement, the same complete occupation of the people. I saw no roughs, loafers, or Arabs. Once, turning a corner, I came on a pair of bare dirty legs, the body which belonged to them being concealed in a doorway. Here is an Arab, thought I. But he was sitting down reading a newspaper.

To go back to the steamer for a minute. We had negro melodists on board, with the banjo and familiar tunes—but the real thing, with wonderful mouths and teeth. I must tell you, too, of the negro barbers in the hairdresser's shop in the ship. I had my hair cut by one, and it was a new sensation. You are laid back in a chair with your legs on a high stool. Sambo is curiously deliberate. He cruises about you with little flips and touches before he begins. Then he scratches your head lazily with his own fingers and slow sympathetic sleepiness. Time is no object to him. He pauses to look out of the window. When he has scratched your head, he brings a dish of rose-water and washes your face, eyes, neck, and ears, with the gentlest and most searching touch possible. He stops to smile on you, and fetch some other bottle of scent. This washing, by the way, is a most exquisite refreshment at a railway station, where Sambo is sure to appear. Then he completes the process with the same smiling gravity, as if you were the last he should ever have the chance of operating on after the manner that he loves. At some places you may have your shoes blacked at the same time that your head is dressed.

At Albany, we, in American phrase, "went on board the train" for Niagara Falls. The train started at 11 P.M. There was a sleeping-car attached to it, with regular beds, pillows, sheets, washing-basins, shoe-blacking, and all the rest of it. I was too sleepy to go to bed, and went off soundly at once, directly I had

taken my place in the first seat, till the next morning.
I woke at a quarter to five, to find myself in a compart-
ment fifty feet long and nine feet high, fitted with

AMERICAN LOCOMOTIVE.

velvet-padded seats, most roomy and comfortable.   A
cord hung along the roof for any passengers to call the
guard.   A street, as it were, runs the entire length of

the train, so that you may walk from one end to the other. I had heard a great deal of the jolting in the American "cars," but I was able to write and read easily. At Syracuse, by five o'clock in the morning boys boarded the train with the newspapers. I bought one, and found extracts from the leaders in the *Times* and other London papers of *the day before*, furnished by the Atlantic Cable; also the Berlin news of the same date. Yet Syracuse, of which I dare say many of our readers never heard before, is only a provincial town. Before six the train was traversed four times by boys selling familiar English novels, periodicals, maps, prints, eatables, &c., &c. They gave you the novel or periodical to read for a few minutes, and then took it away without a word if you did not choose to buy it. There was no pressing to purchase anything. All was done in silence. A man in the next seat to mine opened several packets of prints, looked them over, and laid them down. The boy carried them away without a remark. A carpenter, with trousers patched at the knees, came and sat by me. We had a good deal of conversation. He said that numbers of New England farmers were breaking up their homes to go South, where land was to be bought at a small fractional part of, the price it cost there. He was polite, full of information, and tobacco. At Rochester we stopped to breakfast, elaborately, and found Sambo with the irrepressible rose-water and smiles. The country through which we passed was undulatory, and studded with farms. The farming was coarse, but apparently successful. The cows and sheep were English, the former of Devonshire breed, the latter black-faced. The horses are inferior animals, ewe-necked and leggy. There are no gates or road-keepers at crossings, but a notice in large letters says: "Railway crossing. Look out for the cars." The trains ran naked through part of the town of Rochester, a big bell like a church bell, on the engine, being tolled as we rushed down the streets.

At 12.30 we reached the Niagara Falls. I was quite prepared to be disappointed, but was not. The way in which the river turns slowly over the precipice, like a great green wheel of water, before it thunders down on the rocks below, is most overwhelming. I cannot describe the Falls, or the play of rainbows in the mist, or the gravity of the plunge. There is little noise, but a fulness of sound which you notice in a few minutes. Cataract is too pert a word to use. As a gentleman said to me, the scene was oceanic. After dinner we were rowed across the river in the face of the Falls, and, in oilskin suits, went to the farthest accessible spot, not far, under them. We had to bellow into one another's ears to be heard, and were blinded and drenched for our pains.

CHAPTER III.

NIAGARA TO CHICAGO.

I TRAVELLED through part of Canada on my way, and experienced the sensation of seeing settlements in the state of formation in my route. The settler, his log hut, and heavy labour with the axe, have been so long familiar to my mind's eye, that it was with a sort of anxious curiosity I looked for him in the body. Ay, there it was, when I woke up in the train where I slept, and the morning sun showed a new world going into the crucible of industry. There was the primæval forest right and left, so like an ordinary English wood with coarse grass and undergrowth, that I had to ask myself, "Is this the untouched wild where timber is a 'drug'?" Presently we came to an opening. Yes! there was the log hut, and the settler, axe in hand, was making a clearing. Some trees were down, some were doomed, with the fatal ring cut in their bark about two or three feet from the ground. This soon became a familiar sight. I saw villages where the log hut had passed into a framed house, and the framed house was being superseded by the brick building.

Then came a town, or "city," a straggling set of
tenements through which the train rushed tolling its
bell, and sometimes tooting sharply with its whistle
(only the whistles here are trumpets) to scare some
children off the line, which ran as bare as a path
across a field.

Thus we rushed for some eighteen hours, passing
into Michigan at Detroit. The country was flat and
productive. The crops were mainly of maize. I saw
seed clover and abundance of apple-trees. The wheat
and other corn had been housed. The fields were
studded with the stumps of trees; the fences zigzag—
what they call "snake" or "worm" fences here. It
struck me that Michigan showed a more advanced
civilisation than the part of Canada I had traversed.
There were very few log houses, the towns and villages
looked more prosperous, and the farming was better.
Still it was nature not yet subdued.

As the time-table indicated that we must be drawing
near to it, I began to look out for Chicago, lately a
settlement in the Far West, now a thriving city. I
got out on the platform of the "car" and gazed
eagerly westward. A black cloud hung over the flat
land ahead. "That must be the place," I thought.
My expectations were far exceeded when, after a close
view of Lake Michigan, with its sea-like horizon,
studded with sails and streaked with steamer-smoke,
I plunged into a city with great stone and brick-built

houses, six storeys high, roaring streets as broad as Pall Mall, brimful of strong life, crowded with grand plate-glass-windowed shops, and a tide of men pouring along their sides like the endless processions on the pavements in Cheapside. Thirty years ago there were few better buildings than a log house in Chicago, but they tell me this is the growth of some ten or twelve years. When Lord Palmerston was an elderly man there were some twenty houses, and between 100 and 200 people, in the place. It is now not only a thriving mercantile city, but possesses all the luxuries of civilisation, down to the little nicknacks of artificial ease which you find in Oxford Street. I was long wandering about, bewildered at this miracle of growth. The railway termini astonished me, and the number of rails which enter them. At one, I forget which, I counted the iron rails I stepped over: there were fifty-two. I really cannot tell you how many termini there are. My map says eleven. These pour in grain from a district of prodigious fertility. The produce is not all of grain, though. The stock-yards are a marvel of the place. Pigs are a great item in the trade. They are killed by machinery. One establishment, when in full work, kills and "packs" 2,500 hogs a-day. Piggy is made into pork before he has time to begin squeaking. Peaches, too, are abundant. Some streets were lined with baskets of them, brought from the other side of Lake

Michigan, and about to be sent away. I counted several squares of baskets, and tried to calculate the number which were being packed, but gave it up, and in the course of the evening asked a gentleman to whom I was introduced what the exportation of peaches was. He said that they had sent off about twenty thousand half-bushels in the course of the day. But this is only one small phase of the trade of Chicago.

I was struck with the preponderance of men in the streets, and I hardly saw an old man among them. These Westerners, moreover, are a tall, fine-grown race. Every one is busy, and the people walk faster than in New York. Everything seems being done orderly. There were policemen at the corners with stout sticks in their hands, who made openings in the procession of vehicles for foot-passengers to cross. Much of the city is paved with wood, and more of this pavement is being laid down. They have a curious custom of anchoring the horses here. No one has time to stand at a horse's head, so the driver carries a lump of iron, like a squat four-stone weight, which is fastened by a thong to the bridle. When he stops to load or unload he flings this out, and the horse is what they call "hitched" at once.

But I should not have time to describe the details which strike a stranger. Even the shoe-blacks, though they are behind ours in not working with two brushes at once, seem possessed with an exceptional vigour. They are not content with the familiar importunity of the invitation to " Shine your boots, sir." One morning I was standing at the door of my hotel—the Sherman House—somewhat dust-footed. Blackey, of course, assailed me. I moved on, not wanting him. He ran along on all-fours by my side with flying sweeps and shots at my boots, challenging the verdict of opinion like a true Yankee, and crying, " Won't charge a cent, sir, if you don't like 'em."

I will now, once for all, go back to the railroad and describe the way in which travelling arrangements are made here. I started from Niagara Suspension Bridge at night. I had, following a national custom, previously taken my ticket through to Chicago at an office adjoining the hotel. On reaching the station I was asked if I wanted a sleeping-berth. "Yes," said I, and bought one for the lower tier. Then I handed my luggage to the porter, who hung a brass label to it, giving me a corresponding one. Next I was civilly informed that the sleeping-car would be ready before the train started, so that any one who wanted to go to bed before the car was coupled on might do so. I entered the car, which was about 50 feet long, with two tiers of beds and a pathway between them. They were bonâ fide beds, with pillows, sheets, &c., &c. Mine was about three feet wide and six feet long. It had two double windows looking out of the train, with a handsomely-framed mirror between them. The berth was of dark wood, carved, fitted with electro-plated metal, and had thick-patterned woollen curtains to secure privacy. A number of ladies and gentlemen were my companions in the car, which had a separate washing-place and divers other conveniences at one end. The party of travellers soon melted off into the beds, putting their boots and shoes outside their respective berths.

I did not "turn in" at once, but travelled some time on the platform at the end of the car in conversation with an agreeable American gentleman.

Next morning, after we had all got up, I went on the platform again for the view and fresh air. When I re-entered the car, the beds had all disappeared, as if by magic, being replaced by a number of most comfortable sofas, the top tier having been turned back to the roof, and the sheets, &c., all stowed away by the negro in attendance. American railway tickets are of paper, not card. When in the train my ticket was taken from me, and a card, with the names of the stations and their distances from our starting-place printed upon it, given me instead. Then a notice was hung up stating where we stopped for dinner. At dinner we had some of the ordinary American dishes, with coffee or weak tea. No one took wine or beer. The meal cost 75 cents. As we neared

Chicago the conductor furnished a ticket for the omnibus to the hotel, and took down the destination of my carpet-bag, which in due time made its appearance in my bed-room. There was no asking for "tips," but when I reached the terminus, being freed from all concern about my luggage, I was directed to the first stage or 'bus for the Sherman House, where ready attendants carried in my traps.

Thus you see the traveller is well looked after here. A word as to the defects in American railway travelling. The conductor and guard seemed too indifferent to the breaks. They walked about the train, or sat down to read the paper, though we were running at extra speed to make up for lost time; and I did not see how, if there had been sudden need for them, the breaks could have been applied.

When I got into the hotel a smiling negro came at once into my bed-room to brush American and Canadian dust off my clothes, and suggest a visit to the hairdresser's shop in the hotel, before dinner. At dinner a list of fifty-seven dishes, all ready, and printed for that day's meal, was popped before me, and I sat down at one of sixteen tables, each holding fourteen gentlemen, all of whom appeared to drink only iced water, followed by a cup of coffee.

This is surely a temperate country in the matter of drink. I have sauntered about by night and day in all manner of places, but I have not seen a drunken person, nor have I heard a brawl, though there are hundreds of Lager-beer saloons in the town. These are mainly used by Germans, who sit there often with their families, and listen to music while they smoke, and sip a moderate cup. Of course there is drunkenness here; but in comparing this city of the West, with its young, eager life, to London, the gin-shops of the latter, and their fringe of sots, sorely humbled me.

Near Niagara I had a long talk with a blacksmith who sat by me on a bench, and asked him about the amount of drinking which prevailed. "Sir," said he, "if the foreman knew that one of the men in our shop had got drunk on the *Sunday*, he would be turned out on Monday morning."

On the other hand, a policeman here told me there were divers places where rioting and stabbing went on. That I should have supposed; but, having a tolerably quick eye for rough London life, and wandering late about the streets which were fullest of "saloons," all I can say is, that I saw nothing of any intemperance or disorder.

The arrangements for notice of fire here are excellent. The city is divided into numbered wards, in each of which there are divers means of communication with the City Hall. There men sit day and night by a big bell. When a signal of fire comes, this big bell tolls the number of the ward, so that all the inhabitants know at once where the fire is. Suppose the number of ward in which the fire has broken out is 27, the bell tolls twice for 2, and seven times for 7. If the fire is a large one, this signal is repeated several times. My hotel was close to the City Hall, and the fire signal sounded while I was there. I looked out of my window, an upper one, and saw a number of people get out of their trap-doors on their flat roofs and gaze in the same direction, at once. A man working at a window opposite mine laid down his tools, apparently to count the strokes on the big bell, which were peremptorily repeated. Then his head came up through the roof, and he looked out westward directly; but as the fire seemed to make no show, he went down again to his work.

I must reserve for another chapter what I have seen and learnt of the working of the Church here. The Bishop of Illinois was very kind, favouring me with a long interview and asking me to take part in the services of the cathedral one Sunday, when he had both an Ordination and a Confirmation. I shortly afterwards set off for California, by the new Atlantic and Pacific Railway.

CHAPTER IV.

FROM CHICAGO TO SAN FRANCISCO.

As the train from Chicago did not reach Omaha till
five hours after time, we had our long railway journey
relieved by one night's stoppage in this latter place.
This delay was mainly caused by our having in the
rear of our train an unfinished, but superlatively decorated drawing-room Pullman's car, to be exhibited at
San Francisco, and for the privilege of riding in which
a private party paid a special price. We had not gone
far before all the wheel-boxes grew so hot that we
pulled up to doctor them. This stoppage was repeated so often that we soon lost some hours and
much patience. At last our conductor said, "Guess
it will cool itself running;" and we ran. At about
11 o'clock P.M. a man put his head into my car, which
was next to the splendid defaulter, and cried out,
"The train is on fire!" Then he screwed up the
breaks, which anybody can get at, rang the bell, and
jumped clean off into the night. I went out on the
platform at the end of the car, and found one of the
wheel-boxes in full blaze, and the conductor loosening

the breaks.   He had no notion of stopping then. The man who had given the alarm was a would-be "stowaway," who had caught and climbed up into our train in the dark, and then becoming, or pretending to be, frightened, had acted as I have described. "Confound him!" said our attendant (only he used very much stronger language), "he has nearly stopped the train!"   "What has become of him?" said I, looking down into the road, strewn apparently with logs, into which he had leapt. "Guess he ain't hurt," said the man. "But how about the wheel-box?" I inquired. "Guess we'll put it out at ——" I forget the name of the station.   So we blazed on. Next morning, on awaking at 6, I said to the negro attendant in our car, "How is the box?"   "Guess it's burnt itself out now," said he.

But we were obliged to drop it astern shortly before we reached "Council Bluffs," the station on the east side of the Missouri, Omaha being on the west.   We were detained, however, not only by fire; heavy rain had fallen, and laid part of the road under water. Now, as the rails are nailed to sleepers placed simply on prairie soil, which when wet turns to black mud, we had to go very cautiously for a considerable distance.   The rails were covered with water, but we churned up the mud on either side with such effect, the car next to mine following with foam at its bows like a barge, that every minute we expected to stick

fast.   But we crept through, getting to Council Bluffs
five hours behind our time.   Then, after being ferried
across the Missouri, we ploughed up to this place in
a stage, which at last stood still in a hole, the gentlemen passengers being all obliged to alight.   However,
with four horses, and men at the wheels, we got out.

We were fairly in the West then.   The country
from Chicago to Omaha not long ago was simple
prairie.   Much of it is settled, and we passed many
villages of white wooden houses and scattered farms.
But in Iowa there is still a large tract of land unoccupied.   The soil throughout is deep and black, with
apparently not a stone in it.   There are, however,
occasional mounds of gravelly sand, which seem as if
they had been shed or tilted upon it (is this done by
ice ?), and many small trees, which seem to have
grown since the original prairie was reclaimed.   These
trees, except by the sides of watercourses, almost
ceased as farms became rarer towards Omaha.   The
country is not so flat as it seems to be from a distance, but has gentle undulations.

We had crossed the Mississippi by a very long
wooden bridge.   It was my first sight of that famous
river.   I looked out of the window and saw it suddenly.
A coffee-coloured, smooth-surfaced river, with low
banks.   A large, high-backed white steamboat was
ascending it, like a dirty swan without a neck.

In the train was a party of emigrants ; and I found

that there are three classes on American railways as well as on our own. My ticket was marked " First Class." This, however, became practically second, as I paid something extra for a seat in a Pullman's Palace car. Besides these, there was a car for emigrants. I walked the whole length of the train, and came upon dozens of them, men, women, and children, lying fast asleep on the floor of the carriage. They were near to their new home.

We put down some at a little station with a few wooden houses by it. As we pulled up I saw a fine "Western boy," in broad-brimmed hat and high boots, staring with all his eyes at the car. There tumbled out a woman and three children. "Ah, Bill!" she cried, as she caught sight of the bearded giant; and he hugged and kissed her then and there with enthusiasm. It was a husband who had gone out first to provide a home;—and, for farmers, what a home it is! The first thing they do is to mow the prairie. We saw many stacks of rough hay thus provided. Then comes the plough, turning up the black soil with a cut as clean as that of a knife through butter.

We crossed many streams or rivers, all black, and passed shallow lakes with black rims, and wild-fowl scared by our train. Many herds of cattle, mostly red, grazed knee-deep in the prairie grass. Birds were scarce. I saw swallows, several hawks, two flocks of what seemed to be starlings, but they were not, and some birds like oyster-catchers, flying low and following the course of the streams.

Our company was American, with the exception of an artillery officer from Toronto, whom we presently dropped at Fort Kearney, to shoot buffaloes and elks. He was a very agreeable companion, and I wish he had gone on to San Francisco with me. We talked "Indians" and "buffaloes" late into the evening with an American, in a spare saloon, which we converted into a smoking-carriage. The Indians were, they said, out on the war-path then; lately, they had crossed the line and cut the telegraph wires; but I doubt whether they have tools heavy enough to take up any of the rails.

The Pullman's Palace cars are very comfortable. I had a sofa to myself, with a table and lamp. The sofas are widened and made into beds at night. My berth was three feet three inches wide, and six feet three inches long. It had two windows looking out of the train, a handsome mirror, and was well furnished with bedding and curtains. Some of the passengers went to bed with great orthodoxy.

I do not believe that hotel cars are run every day for ordinary passengers on the Pacific Railway. Sometimes a party charters one, but they are really little better than the ordinary Palace cars. As there are plenty of stations where food is procured, the train stops for breakfast, dinner, and supper. It is well, however, to be furnished with some additional provisions, as, from the specimens we have already had, the punctuality of the stoppages is not to be altogether depended upon.

The Missouri is yellow, with many shifting sandbanks. Its waters were very low, in spite of the rain. I was told that we should reach dry regions as the road rose towards the Rocky Mountains. We were soon to enter on the great plains of Nebraska, and a gentleman who had lately traversed the whole route said that the track was much better westward than we had found it as yet. Omaha was then the muddiest place I ever saw, and the number of dirty boots with legs inside them tilted up round the stove in the office below—where the clerk, too, had his heels on his desk when I fetched my oil lamp to go to bed by—was enough to gladden the heart of the yawning negro who acts as shoeblack, for he charged 15 cents a pair. They say, however, that mud is rare in Omaha. The roads are generally deep with dust. The men, apparently far outnumbering the women, are mostly tall, strapping fellows, with broad-brimmed hats, and blue trousers stuck into their boots. The houses, as a rule, are of wood, painted white. The main street was, when I saw it, a slough, navigated by one car on rails, which plied perpetually up and down. The horses were excellent, and splashed to their ears.

At Omaha we took the train for San Francisco direct, and, with the exception of an occasional stoppage for a few minutes, and two hours at Promontory, travelled day and night for nearly five days, or 110 hours.   Before very long we found ourselves in the prairie; and, as the freshest impressions are sometimes the best, I will here copy a letter which I wrote home from the train, at one of the convenient little tables with which the car was furnished :—

" I now date from the train, and you can see by my writing that we travel with considerable steadiness. We are passing through the prairie.   On my right hand as I look out of the window I see an ocean of coarse hay-grass ; this is broken to my left by a few scattered trees which mark the course of the North Platte River, which we have followed for a long distance.   Beyond the river the grass appears again and stretches to the horizon, unbroken by any tree, but undulating like the Atlantic with a heavy ground-swell.   The prairie is much like what I expected to see, though the grass is shorter than I thought it was ; but the continual progress through a boundless plain without a hedge or mark of any sort produces an impression it is hard to describe.   You almost think the train must be standing still, and that you are looking at the small section of a hayfield which could be seen through a window.   But the talk in the train is that the buffaloes are coming north for this

RAILWAY STATION, PROMONTORY POINT.

short, sweet grass, and the Indians after them. In
writing this last sentence I am appropriately reminded
that the view from my car is laid in no long-civilised
park, for I look up and see a bouâ fide Indian, in
paint and Indian dress, who has alighted from his
horse by the roadside, and is staring at the train and
smoking a pipe. I have laid down my pen for a few
minutes, and take it up again to remark that the view
over the prairie from the right-hand window of my
car has become more striking. The horizon is perfectly flat, and the most distant portion of the plain
exactly resembles the sea. Several of my companions,
who, like me, have never seen this sight before, are
now looking out of the car and talking of the perfect
resemblance of the prairie horizon to that of water.
The waving of the grass under the wind adds to the
deception. We have just passed a herd of antelopes."

At the risk of a certain amount of repetition, I will
reserve for the next chapter a more consecutive account of our journey. Now I will give you merely
general impressions. We reached San Francisco
safely in five days. The whole of the railroad to
this city was really not quite finished, but from
Omaha to Sacramento was in excellent order. True,
the wooden bridges over the cañons (pronounced
canyons) were temporary, and looked from a distance
as if they were built of lucifer matches. The trains
creep slowly over them, and they creak terribly; but

on the solid ground the road-bed is firm, the track smooth, the time fairly kept, the attendance good, and the provision at the stopping-places on the line excellent, considering the difficulties which must be met in supplying it. We ran through more than 1,000 miles from Omaha to Promontory, a place so called because it juts out into the Great Salt Lake. Then we entered the cars of the Central Pacific, which we did not quit till we reached Sacramento. This latter portion of the line is made by Chinese. We passed scores of these "navvies," in Chinese suits, long pigtails, and hats like crushed beehives.

When we reached Sacramento we were shifted to the new line, 134 miles long, between that place and San Francisco. It was not yet completed, since we had to take the ferry across the bay for half-an-hour. Indeed, part of that which we passed over was not made when we reached it. The sleepers were flung upon the ground; the rails, however, were not only not fastened down, but not even laid in their places. As the train stopped I looked out of a window, and became aware of a mixed party of Irishmen and Chinese hammering, digging, shouting, cackling (Chinese cackle), in advance of us. I stepped out and walked on, to find the line in the state I have described.

Lighting my cigar and sitting down on the trunk of a tree by the road-side, I saw it finished in an hour,

at high pressure. A quarter of a mile, at the very
least, including a portion over a long bridge, was laid
as fast as ever the rails could be steadied on the
sleepers, with the greatest economy of nails. At last
a chief Paddy laid down the hammer which he had
been wielding with the precision and force of a small
steam-engine, and shouted out, "Come along wid
ye!" And we came, a train of ten cars. Then the
engine-driver said, "Is it all right further on?" "All
right," said Paddy; and away we went, 25 miles an
hour, presently, under a full moon so bright that on
stopping at one of the stations I was enabled to read
a book by it. But the road was decidedly rough.
"Rough!" said one of my Yankee companions;
"cussed if I think there is any track at all; it goes
like a scared bullock."

I am bound, however, to say that this is the only
portion of the great Atlantic and Pacific line to which
such language could be applied. This will soon be
put into good order, and the rest is as smooth and
firm as could be wished. Indeed, it showed a very
marked contrast to the Chicago and North-Western,
by which I travelled to Omaha. A word about the
cars before I proceed to attempt some detailed de-
scription of this wonderful route. Those on the first
part from Omaha to Promontory are decidedly the
best. The Pullman hotel cars were not then running
on the line for ordinary passengers, but were expected

to do so in about a fortnight. We brought the inflammable Drawing-room Palace car with us after all. It heated two or three times west of Omaha, but had to succumb to the exigencies of its position, and ran well the rest of the way. For a time, though, we thought it would mar our journey, for we had to make up the time spent in doctoring it, and special speed is not pleasant. But all went right, and a very agreeable gentleman, who is connected with the Company and travelled in it, met our murmuring with much good temper. I came in a "Pullman's Palace sleeping car." It held twelve bottom and twelve upper berths, the former of which were converted into sofas during the day. There was a washing place, &c., at one end, and the berths were more roomy than in the "Silver Palace cars" of the Central Pacific. The track, however, on both portions of the line is equally good, which is commendable, considering the pace at which it was made. Indeed, for some hundred miles in the middle of the Great Rocky Mountain desert the lines were pushed on with such a speed that they overshot each other. The object of each rival company was to get as many rails laid as possible. They were each to enjoy the Government grant up to the spot where they met in working order. Thus the lines were graded—*i.e.*, prepared for the sleepers and rails—as far on in advance of their actual completion as they could be ; and, as I said, when we got into the cars of

the Central Pacific we passed some 100 miles, it may
be more or less, of the Atlantic and Pacific, which
could not be covered with sleepers and rails before the
line was met, with an engine upon it. The lines run
in some places within a few yards of each other, and
imagination must be left to picture the comments of
the Irish navvies on the Chinese as they worked in
rivalry almost side by side. There is no good feeling
between these classes of labourers. We came in one
place to the charred remains of some railway works,
and on inquiring the cause of them I was told that
they were burnt because they had been built by
Chinese. But the " children of the sun " are content
to work hard if they can earn money, and I suppose
do not feel the degradation of a kick. Certainly,
nothing could be more cheerful than their manner
·when they crowded, as they did in one or two places,
to exchange many signs and a few English words with
the passengers in the train. The greeting from the
cars was, " John ! build railway ? " " Tchess," says
John, nodding and grinning. "Good," says Uncle
Sam ; and that was about all they had to-say to each
other.

The company " on board " our train was almost
entirely American. I have mentioned that we carried
an English artillery officer to a small station about
six miles from Fort Kearney, where he was turned
out with his rifle in his hand, a fur coat, a bag, and

good store of Cavendish tobacco, to shoot buffaloes and elks on the prairie. He was quite alone, but counted on making the acquaintance of some United States officers at the fort. It was rather touching, though, leaving him there as we did in the dark, especially as we heard that a tribe of Indians, out for mischief, had crossed the line a night or two before and taken the direction which he intended to pursue. Six companies, with some friendly Pawnees, were reported to have left in pursuit of them that day. "Ever been out in the plains, sir?" said a passenger to this gentleman. "No," replied he quietly. I was glad to find, when I got out of the train to shake hands with him as he departed on his errand, that he had already made friends with an American officer who, with six soldiers, was guarding the station.

We saw no other Englishmen till we reached Promontory, where three came on board from Salt Lake, but left us before we had crossed the Sierra. The rest of our passengers, including divers ladies and children, were very agreeable. A week's journey in the same train makes many friends. Railway travelling in America is much less tedious than in England, You can walk about, stand on the platform at either end of the cars, and make visits to other parts of the train. The engine even is accessible, though I suspect this is rather a stretch. Descending the Sierra Nevada, however, where the sharpest curves occur, and the train, steam being shut off, runs by its own weight down 6,000 feet into the Sacramento Valley, I made friends with the driver, and got a seat by his side. The line is perhaps most interesting here, and I much enjoyed the descent, my intelligent new friend pointing out the various surface gold mines as we passed, and other features of the road.

As for the rest, time was wiled away by cards, conversation, and reading. We had an abundant supply of books and newspapers. A boy frequently traversed the train with a good store of novels, mostly English, periodicals, &c. Even at Chyenne, a place seemingly built half of canvas on the prairie, at the foot of the Rocky Mountains, and exhibiting a dangerous-looking population of miners, &c., in big boots, broad-brimmed hats, and revolvers, the *Chyenne Leader* of that morning, which I bought, and which now lies open before me, had an extract from a leader in the *Times* on the Œcumenical Council at Rome, dated the day before, and news that heavy storms had prevailed throughout England. The way in which the Atlantic Cable is used by the American Press in the most unlikely places, goes to show one phase of the hunger for reading which affects our brethren on this side of the Atlantic; but English books and mere extracts from English newspapers are not the only signs of English literature one meets with here. The first publication I saw on the first bookstall I met with in San Francisco was *Punch*.

I must make use of the jottings and consecutive wayside notes of my route and journey in another chapter. The country we traversed was even wilder than I had expected. With the exception of the thriving Mormon villages and farms in the Great Salt Lake Valley, we seemed to pass through a desert, that portion of it between Chyenne and the Sierra being in many places most dreary, and even in a sense awful, with its lifeless alkaline plains. We rushed through these hour after hour, the lips of the passengers in some cases becoming almost sore with the dry soda dust which we whirled up from the white snow-like soil traversed by the train.

CHAPTER V.

THE GREAT RAILROAD.

ABOUT two-thirds of the American continent are traversed by the road, which has only one line of rails. The plains that come first rise almost imperceptibly from Omaha to an altitude of 7,040 feet above the sea-level in 516 miles, when Chyenne, at the foot of the Rocky Mountains, is reached. Then the ascent is rapid to Sherman, the highest elevation, which *Bancroft's Guide*, from which I take my figures, puts at 8,424 feet, 33 miles distant from Chyenne. From Sherman there is high barren table mountain land for about 500 miles farther, when the Great Salt Lake Valley is reached, with an elevation of 4,320 feet. The road rises again from this to a height of between 6,000 and 7,000, and then drops to about 4,000 before it crosses the Sierra, at an elevation of 7,042. From the summit of this range the descent to Sacramento is rapid, the train running down mainly by its own weight to the sea-level in 105 miles, some parts of this road being much steeper than others. Steam is used for about 30 miles of this distance.

With Sacramento level ground is reached; the length of the combined Atlantic and Pacific and Central Pacific lines being—from Omaha to Sacramento 1,774 miles, and to San Francisco 1,908. 154 stations are marked in my guide-book, many of them being mere tanks for watering the engine, with sometimes only a tent beside them. The express trains do not stop at all of these. Nothing which deserves the name of a town, though some are called cities, is seen between Omaha and Sacramento. Chyenne, the largest, has not emerged from the board and canvas stage, and divers others consist of tents. There are, however, solid erections in several places for the purposes of the railway, and a few of these will in time grow into permanent towns; but a long portion of the route is so hopelessly barren that I doubt if it will ever do more than carry the track.

We left Omaha at nine o'clock one Wednesday morning. At first the country showed much the same degree of civilisation seen the other side of the Missouri, but in about four hours the farms died away, with the exception of some adventurous dots of houses, which were dropped on the outskirts of the settlements. These, however, soon ceased, and we ran in a perfectly straight track, with an interminable row of telegraph posts by our side, across the prairie. I have already described its appearance. Its horizon so closely resembled the sea that it was hard to believe we were looking over a plain which, in time, will be ploughed and reaped. Here is a prospective cornfield some 500 miles wide and 1,000 long. It is impossible to forecast the future of Kansas, Nebraska, and the watered regions north and south of them, into which the tide of agricultural emigration is creeping from Europe and the Eastern States. New England finds for itself a yet newer life in these inexhaustibly fertile territories, still mainly occupied by the Indian, the elk, and the buffalo. "A big country, ours," said several of my companions to me over and over again, with an air of satisfaction which could not have been greater if they had made it themselves. But it is not the bigness which makes it precious. The British possessions to the north of it are as large. Its soil and sun and rivers give it worth and a weight which the Union must be trimmed carefully to carry. I do not say that throughout the whole route I came across any serious sentiment of independence, but distant California, with its gold and grain, sneers and swears at greenbacks. "I know nothing," said a prosperous man to me in the train, "of promises to pay;" and wayside fruitsellers, to whom I, having then no specie, offered notes for pears, &c., cursed them with a will. But most of the Americans with whom I conversed were apparently united at heart.

The sun set over the prairie before our first night in the train, shining last upon a western cloud till it looked like a firmament of gold. Lamps were lit; cards, reading, and conversation still went on in the little slice of civilisation which was rushing through the prairie, now stopping at a station—where the soldiers who guarded it came on board and begged for any papers we could spare, and told us how not long ago they had had a brush with the Indians, and, to use their own words, "taken sixty scalps"—and then scaring antelopes into the safe darkness of distance. At last the attendant came round to convert the sofas into beds, and let down the upper berths. It was an odd experience, that going to bed of some thirty ladies, gentlemen, and children, in, practically, one room. For two nights I had a young married couple sleeping in the berth above mine. The lady turned in first, and presently her gown was hung out over the rail to which her bed curtains were fastened. But further processes of unrobing were indicated by the agitation of the drapery which concealed her nest. As the same curtain served for both berths—hers and mine—the gentleman held her portion together over my head when it was necessary for me to retire. At last all were housed, and some snores rose above the rattle of the train. I did not sleep much the first night, but looked over the moonlit prairie from my pillow. We were then passing through the great buffalo country. Before the week was spent, however, we had all become as used to the exigencies of our position as if we **had** been born and bred in a Pullman's car. The ladies slid **out of** their berths in a very tumbled toilet, and, getting **out** their combs, toothbrushes, and sponges, did such deliberate justice to their charms as circumstances would permit.

On Thursday morning I woke early, to see the grass on the plains shorter, and the ground broken by juttings of rock. It was bitterly cold, and I was very glad of the red blanket with which my berth was furnished. I looked out of the window and saw a string of antelopes cantering off in the early sunshine. If you have never dressed on your back in a box two feet high, you can, at least, suppose that it is inconvenient to do so.

We breakfasted at Chyenne, and had tea, coffee, antelope, beef, mutton, trout, ham, eggs, &c. This is the current bill of fare on the line. The chops were generally as tough as hanks of whipcord, and the knives as blunt as bricklayers' trowels. One of our hosts told me that he kept three fishermen and two hunters to provide food for the trains. I told him I wished he would keep his meat a little, too. No wine or beer was seen till we reached Promontory, when Californian claret made its appearance. We had weak tea with our dinner.

I might as well tell you here something about American cookery. It is rather unintelligible. Gumbo

INTERIOR OF A DRAWING-ROOM CAR (FROM A PHOTOGRAPH).

soup, hominy, squash pie, sweet potatoes, and corn
heads boiled whole, seem to be favourite dishes. The
beef is good, the mutton not so well-flavoured as ours.
Turkey appears everywhere, and eggs have a hundred
forms. The bread is not hearty; the tea is bad.
Claret is reasonably cheap, but, with this exception,
the price of wines is prodigious. Nobody calls for
port or sherry. Most people drink only iced water at
meals. Oysters are abundant, and dressed in countless ways. Clam soup is excellent. Breakfast is
made a great meal of in America, and is, correctly,
on the eastern side of the continent, finished with
huge slices of melon. In California you eat melon
before your proper breakfast is brought. There are
great stalls of peaches in the streets, but they are
not half so good as ours in England. Meals are
taken early. Each guest has a separate dish of what
he calls for. No extra charge is made for ice-creams,
&c. : the waiter puts a whole shape before you, and
you may take what you like. The ices are better
than ours.

Our stopping-place for breakfast was the point of
departure for divers of our fellow-passengers to Denver
and the mines in Colorado. We took up also several
miners for the Sweetwater Gold Mines in Wyoming,
the stages for which left the route at Bryan. It was
curious to see a rough-booted, broad-brimmed fellow
strutting up and down the train with his revolver

slung behind him like a short blunt tail. The breaksman of our train said to me, "Ah, sir, we don't
care for Indians: these boys on the line are more
dangerous; you are obliged to be very careful: there
is no law here. I always carry a revolver." But, of
course, if you leave them alone they don't meddle
with you. They only shoot their friends and acquaintances, as a rule. I was entertained with a conversation between two of them which I happened to
overhear óne day in my car. The first words I caught
were, "Well, sir, I must say you are a curious
individual; I always pull on my man first." "You
see," replied his companion, "it happened thus. I
was dining"—he mentioned some place known to
them both—"and there were two dogs fighting in
the room. So I kicked them out and sat down
again. He"—this referred to some acquaintance—
"you know him; well, he came up and said, 'I hope
you enjoy your dinner.' 'Yes,' says I, 'but why?'
'Well,' says he, 'one of them dogs was mine, and as
sure as you live that is the last dinner you will ever
eat. I'll shoot you down as soon as you cross the
threshold.' Well, so I finished my dinner and went
out. Sure enough he let fly at me, but he was too
close: I knocked his hand up, and the ball went into
the ceiling. So I ran back into the parlour and called
the missus. 'Missus,' says I, 'will you lend me a
pistol?' So she fetched one out of a drawer, but

it warn't no good—one of them little things. So I
bolted out as quick as I could, for I knew there was
a friend of mine t'other side of the road who would
lend me a good 'un. Well, he let fly at me again
and missed, but I got into "—he mentioned the name
of his friend's house—"and then I . . . ." Here,
some noise made me lose the exact end of the story,
but I gathered that he got a good pistol and shot the
owner of the dog.

Several of my companions of this sort were entertaining fellows. I had a good deal of talk with some,
and heard the ups and downs of mining adventure :
how such and such a mine, now of incalculable worth,
was sold for a pistol; how such and such members of
my informant's party were shot by Indians : how he,
in a place he pointed out, had himself shot so and so.
Some gentlemen in the train were fountains of tobacco-
juice, and one in remarkably full play was pointed
out to me as a leading member of his state government. I talked to him as he sat with his legs cocked
up over the back of a sofa. "Been to such and such
a mine, sir," said he, "and it's dusty; look here ; "
and he slapped the leg of his trousers, which gave out
a white cloud around him as if he had patted a flour
sack.

The sun grew hot with the day, and we reached the
highest elevation in the Rocky Mountains crossed by
the train, at about 11. The engine panted slowly up

to this, but the road presented no great engineering difficulties. The summit reached, we took a northerly direction through a bleak country covered with a number of granite heaps, in many cases exactly resembling the tors on Dartmoor. The old emigrant road frequently showed itself to the right or the left, and we passed a toiling team of Mormons on their way to the Great Salt Lake. We got to Laramie at twenty minutes after 12, and, crossing the Laramie plains, over which the Rocky Mountains showed grandly on our left, spent the rest of the day in passing through a miserable wilderness, broken by edges of strata, and occasionally spotted with the skulls, skeletons, and withered carcases of cattle that had perished in crossing them.

Towards evening patches of alkaline soil began to show themselves, and I could in some slight measure imagine the privations to which the emigrants are exposed who cross this region on foot. It is not barren, however, in all senses, for it abounds with coal, and at Carbon (well named) we fed the engine straight from the mine, shortly afterwards passing through strata of coal, which cropped out above the surface of the ground. We crossed the North Platte again near Rawlings, at 6 P.M., by a temporary bridge of timber, which looked unpleasantly fragile, but, being traversed slowly, carried us well over. These trestle bridges are common. They are to be replaced by firmer structures, but answered their purpose. Some creaked as if they were made of wickerwork.

The view over the broken plains by moonlight, which lit up their patches of white soda soil, was very striking, but the dust was painfully unpleasant. The only herbage consisted of sage grass or brush. When the construction train was engaged upon this region, water had to be fetched from a considerable distance, and the names of two of the stations, "Bitter Creek" and "Salt Wells," indicated the destitution of the route.

We woke up early on Friday, to the same high, broken, dreary plains; but there was a little eatable grass. We passed a party of Indians with their squaws and children in full paint, and the lamest horses I ever saw in my life. The streams which we accompanied flowed down towards the Great Salt Lake. We had crossed the watershed of the Rocky Mountains, and at about 9 A.M. reached Echo Cañon, with high red granite cliffs on our right hand, snow-patched mountains having previously shown themselves on our left. Echo was soon reached, and we entered Weber Cañon at 10 A.M. This is a fine gorge. We followed a bright, tumbling stream, passing the "1,000-mile tree," and running through a gap called the Devil's Gate, into a wide, flat bottom, like some parts of the Valley of the Rhone, at 11. This was the beginning of the Great Salt Lake Valley, the

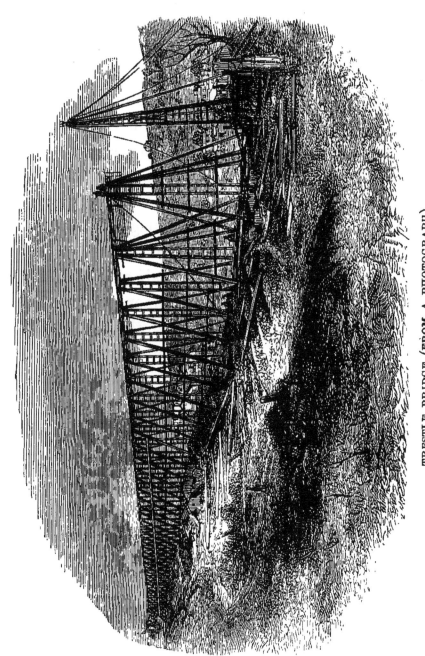

TRESTLE BRIDGE (FROM A PHOTOGRAPH).

mountains which surround it soon showing themselves
in beautiful variety of shape and colour. Here a
revelation awaited us. We came shortly upon the
shore of the lake. Smiling farms, neat small stations,
white and brown cottages, children selling melons and
milk, squared fields, English stacks, herds of cattle,
trim fences, appeared as if by magic—a cheerful
contrast to the wilderness through which we had
passed. The bright blue waves of the lake, the finely-
formed mountains around, with villages nestling at
their foot, and little streams brought down from their
inner stores of fresh water, gave an air of loveliness to
the whole scene. This was Mormon Land. The
mountain streams, led hither and thither, have made
it what it is. The dreary sage grass was passing
away for the cornfield, but the absence of timber still
showed one great want of the land. The settlers,
however, have planted fruit trees extensively; and
each cottage has its orchard of pears, peaches, and
apples. Now this healthy-looking, busy, English-
chattering crowd at the station, with ladies in parasols
and chignons, was Mormon. Say what we will about the
errors of Brigham Young, I could not but honour the
wisdom which had recognised the depth of soil that
lay under this plain—whose surface was in many
places whitened with saline incrustations, but was
rendered fertile with fresh water drawn from the
hills—and the perception of beauty which had led

him to choose so lovely a surrounding for his converts.

We stopped at a station where a party of emigrants had just arrived. Their luggage lay on the ground. The children were playing about, the men and women standing in groups or sitting on their trunks and boxes, gazing on the bright blue lake with its fringe of mountain, which they had reached at last. It must have seemed a paradise to them. I cannot convey to you the sense of relief with which the eye looked upon cornfields, cottages, and glittering ripple after only two days' prospect of dry desolation. We skirted the water for a few hours, and then the wilderness came upon us again on our way to the Sierra Nevada, and I think the moonlight journey of the next night and the whole of the succeeding day revealed as barren a prospect as I ever beheld. True, we ran partly by the Humboldt, which irrigates a narrow strip of land, and has a few ranches, with some herds of cattle and horses, by its side; but the predominant scenery was most desolate, the river itself at last disappearing into the ground. Hour after hour we looked from our windows upon the dry sage-brush-covered waste, and the dry mountain-tops beyond it. There was no life to speak of on the plains. We saw a few herdsmen on horseback, with broad hats and Mexican stirrups; and once, when we stopped at a small station for water, a party of

hideously painted Indian squaws, with brown, half-
naked children, came up to beg.   But they begged
with little energy, holding out their hands in silence
for scraps of food, which they clutched after a half-
shy, half-savage fashion.

The real natives of the country appeared to be
Chinese, who have built the railway eastward up to
the Salt Lake.   We soon found ourselves among
these, and passed many of their encampments, outside of which in the evening they were cooking and
chattering in groups.   I should say that the upper
part of the Salt Lake, which is over 100 miles long
and 35 wide, is skirted by unreclaimed, dreary white
wastes of saline crust, similar, I imagine, to those
seen on the borders of the Dead Sea.   It lies at an
elevation of somewhat more than 4,000 feet above the
ocean-level.   The City of the Saints lies about 30
miles off the line, and was reached by stages from
Uintah.   A railway, however, has now been built to
replace the road.

I saw no boat on the lake, but there were many
gulls, and cattle grazed in the saltings close to its
edge.   It smells much like the Essex marshes, though
a gentleman in the train fancied there was a sul-
phureous taint in the air.   It was only by thinking
about it and sniffing that I detected the saline odour
of the breeze.   The people looked very healthy.

We passed through a God-forsaken-looking country

all that Friday night, and dropped one poor fellow near a ranche, but far from anything like a village. I did not know why the train was stopped, or I suppose I should have given him a dollar or so. I was taking my evening stroll up the train about 9 P.M.; the moon was shining brightly, and I had stopped on the platform of one of the forward cars, when we pulled up and set down a man with a blanket rolled up on his shoulder. I heard him say, "I've had nothing to eat since——." Then he added, to the guard, "Much obliged for your politeness. I've got a dollar." "That won't help you much," said the man; "get down." So he got down, and we were off before I realised that the poor wretch had been dropped in the wilderness, having been found out in the attempt to ride without a ticket.

It was bitterly cold when I awoke the next morning (Saturday) to find the train still in the same horrible desert. We parted with a crowd of miners at Elko for the White Pine district, where, they say, silver can be cut out of the rock with a chisel. The riches of this district are concealed under a forbidding outside. People said that the mineral wealth of the region through which we were passing was incalculable, but comparatively untouched. Hour after hour we rushed on through the sage-brush plains skirted by these precious mountains. We saw a few wandering Shoshones. The alkaline dust annoyed us again,

and my finger nails by this time had become quite
brittle.   We were all in a wearisome humour through
this day, and were glad to get to bed.

Early next morning (Sunday) we found ourselves
ascending the Sierra by a number of sharp curves.
The steepest gradient is 116 feet in the mile, and
some curves have a radius of only 600 feet.   There
are, they say, 40 miles of curves with a radius of less
than 1,000 feet.   In some places the train seemed to
make an half-circle.   It was freezing sharply on the
summit.   Rumour asserts that political interests have
taken the line over a needlessly difficult ridge, and
that a much better pass could have been found to San
Francisco if Sacramento had not insisted on being
made the first terminus of the line.

The scenery to the right, where several lakes show
themselves far below the track, is very beautiful; but
it is spoilt by the snow-sheds, which cover the line for
some forty miles, and afford only glimpses of the
country far beneath the traveller.   These sheds are
made of sawed pine timber, covered with plank, and
a more convenient arrangement for a long bonfire I
never saw.   This part of the line must be burnt some
day, as the chimney of every engine goes fizzing
through it like a squib, and the woodwork is as dry as
a bone.

For some time from the summit we passed through
mountains wholly covered with pine and cedar, and

ran carefully round the heads of valleys and spurs of the range. As I have said, steam was shut off, and men were put at all the breaks. It struck me that there was greater care shown by the officials in this part of our route. The breaksmen and conductors had hitherto smoked and chewed whenever they could, which was almost always; but when I offered a cigar to a fresh Californian breaksman here he said, "Thank you, sir, but it's against the rules to smoke while on duty."

Presently we came down to sawmills and cows, the effect being strikingly Swiss when the Chinese were not in sight. Then we reached the surface gold mines, where the soil on both sides was pitted with diggings, and many water-troughs led streams for the miners to wash for the metal. At last we got a glimpse of the yellow Californian plain, and soon found ourselves on the flats—park-like breadths of grass and cornland, studded with scrub oaks and blazing in the sunshine. We reached Sacramento—a hot, dusty town—between 12 and 1. Magnificent pears, grapes, &c., were offered at the left hand window of our train, while on the right we saw the yellow river with its white steamboats. Here we were shifted to the cars of the unfinished portion of the rail, and took ten hours to reach San Francisco, though the distance traversed is only 134 miles. Part of the route lay over a perfectly flat plain covered with cornfields and cattle, and skirted by distant hills on either side, the

F

river lying some distance off on our right. The value of these plains is increasing yearly; they are very extensive, one corn valley alone leading off from them with a flat bottom 17 miles wide and nearly 200 long. A few years ago these priceless fields could have been secured on the Government terms of a dollar and a-quarter an acre. Not only is the soil rich and deep, but the farmer may be sure of sunshine during harvest. The corn is not even put into sheaves, but gathered up to the steam threshing machine from where it lies. The straw is burnt, as no one thinks of using manure. Towns and villages are springing up like beds of mushrooms along the railway which traverses this precious district, and already the Californian sells his wheat at a profit in Liverpool.

The latter part of the road lies through a country of mounds, and a ferry is taken across the bay for half-an-hour to San Francisco. We left a straight wake in the smooth bay, as under a glorious moon we steamed towards the twinkling lights of the city, having the Golden Gate or entrance to the harbour on our right. It was past 11 when I reached my hotel, but, though so late, I got at once what the sense of a week's racket, accumulated soda dust, and engine smoke, had made me long for—a delicious, roomy warm bath—and enjoyed a chamber more than two feet high. I will tell you something about San Francisco in my next chapter.

CHAPTER VI.

SAN FRANCISCO.

THIS is, I should think, the most hilly town in the world. Laid out in squares, like other American cities, almost every vista presents a slope, with sometimes a gradient of one in six, inasmuch as the ground on which it is built is simply a collection of steep sandhills. The inconvenience of this is, of course, very great; and though it may be a fine thing in theory to defy the ups and downs of nature and show a map as rectangular as that of Philadelphia, the San Franciscans are beginning to make cuttings in their city. This, however, leaves the houses which lined the street high up in the air. I called on the Bishop of California one afternoon. The " Directory " said he lived at 348 Second Street. So I went to Second Street, and found in the part where his house ought to have been, a fresh-made cliff, 50 feet high, on either side, and a crowd of navvies carting away stuff. It was impossible to reach the Bishop's nest from the street, so I beat round to get to the back of it. On arriving at the spot I asked where the Bishop lived.

"The Bishop?" said a jolly-looking gentleman to
me; "why, his house has tumbled down into the street.
But come with me: I know some one who will tell
you where he has gone to." And he turned into a
bar, saying, "Sir, what will you drink?" It is
mortal offence to refuse such an invitation, so I "put
a name" to some American liquid. "Now, then,"
said he to the bar-keeper, "tell the gentleman where
the Bishop lives;" and I found that he had flitted to
the other end of the city, but I had to go elsewhere
for his address.

One advantage, if it be such, in this perpendicular
style of architecture, is that in whichever direction
you walk you soon have a bird's-eye view of the place.
It is well situated on the bay; but the beach, at least
that portion of it frequented by the inhabitants, is
some six miles off. The shore of the bay by the
town is full of busy wharves, and set thick with
masts. The hotels, churches, and other public
buildings in the centre of San Francisco, have large
pretensions, some of them being really very fine; but
as the city stretches out in readiness to grow to any
size, the streets soon pass into steep sandy roads, in
which the wind makes deep drifts, and the wheels of
the "spider waggons" common in America sink half-
way up to the axle. Many street cars ply in the most
navigable thoroughfares. As usual, there are no
cabs, but lumbering "silver-plated" hackney coaches

with two horses, for riding in one of which from the landing-stage of the ferry to the hotel I was charged two dollars and a-half.

The pavement of Montgomery Street, the chief thoroughfare, is thronged by crowds of men who all seem busy and in the prime of life. It combines business and pleasure, being at once the Wall Street and Broadway of the city. Every nation and tongue has representatives here. Californians, merchants and miners, Mexicans—I have seen them, with high-peaked saddle and lasso, riding by—negroes, the broadest. Irish, Germans, and Chinese make up the multitude. Sudden fortunes bring the miner into the best hotels. The man sitting near you at dinner may be well dressed, but he may have hands horny and brown as a navigator's, and a navigator's appetite. In the same room, perhaps at the same table, are elegant Californian belles. The way in which society, as seen in the streets and inns, is jumbled up here, is very striking. But though there are evil-looking, underground, gas-lit saloons, in which sirens sit to greet any visitor, close to the best hotels, the behaviour of the people in the streets is outwardly decent, and you seldom see a policeman.

The quarter of the Chinese up Sacramento Street is very curious. They live here in thousands, and have made a portion of the city almost their own, having theatres and joss-houses, or temples, where they play and pray in the most orthodox national fashion. I spent many hours in prowling and shopping among them. They say you may buy rats to eat, but most unpleasant-looking pork seems to be their chief meat. All is done after Chinese ways. The signs of the shops are written and the books kept in Chinese. I bought a pair of shoes and a wonderful hat of "Wo Cum," who tied up my parcel with a strip of grass, and entered the transaction at the wrong end of a rice-paper book, with a brush dipped in Indian ink rubbed on a saucer, in complicated letters an inch square. Then I wanted a Chinese coat. He showed me a silk one. "Inglis good," said Wo Cum. "No," replied I; "no Inglis, give Chinaman's." And he despised me for buying one of native fabric and manufacture.

I was very anxious to see a joss-house. Californians seem to treat such places with contempt, and I asked in vain some half-dozen persons whether they could direct me to one. So I went into the shop of "Loo Sing," who, far from being jealous of a Christian going to see his house of prayer, sold me, nodding and smiling, a bundle of joss-sticks, things like thin bulrushes, made of pastil, and burnt before idols. Then said I, adopting his own Chinese English, "Want see joss-house, Chinaman's god." "Oh! ah! Tchess," said John, grinning; "I show." But even when he had directed me to the right corner of the street I was still at a loss, seeing nothing but ordinary houses. At last I caught a passing China-man, and made him take me to the sanctuary. It was approached through a shop. We went up-stairs and along a passage; then he waved his hand as he led me into a good-sized darkened chamber, where I found myself for the first time in my life in the pre-sence of real heathen idolatry. The air was heavy with incense. An altar, some 8 feet by 3 feet, and 3 feet high, draped in embroidered cloth, with two mats for kneeling before it, stood at one end of the chamber. It had upon it two burning lamps with slender stems, two candlesticks, a vessel with smoul-dering incense, and two vases of artificial flowers. Immediately behind it, in a shallow recess, was the idol, with drapery concealing all but the small wooden face of a doll, whose dark hair was parted in the middle. At the first glance there was little to dis-tinguish what I saw from a dirty altar in a dark Roman Catholic chapel. The incense, the drapery, the vases of artificial flowers, the burning lamps, the joss-sticks of worshippers stuck in front like tapers, and the wooden shrouded doll, at once illustrated an anecdote, which I had disbelieved, of a Chinaman who visited a Jesuit chapel, and came out, saying, "Good, joss-house same." "This Chinaman's god?" said I to my guide. "Tchess," replied he, "Chinaman's god;" and some new thoughts came into my mind.

I visited the Chinese theatre, and was fortunate in being present on a benefit night, when the entertainment was wholly for the Chinese. I was the only white man present, with the exception of a policeman in plain clothes, who turned out to be a native of my own county, Suffolk, in England. I gave him a cigar, which he smoked then and there while on duty.

The play was so far intelligible that it involved love and jealousy. The theatre was crammed; the actors who did not play in the piece sitting on either side of the stage. There was apparently a religious element in the drama, for an altar stood in the middle of the stage, and the two chief performers, dressed in long straight embroidered robes, with loose sleeves, knelt down before it for a minute with their backs to the audience. There appeared to be an Emperor and his Queen, who quarrelled because of some attentions paid by the former to a young lady, who sang a song accompanied by a gong, bones, and a sort of fiddle. The Queen pulled the Emperor's beard, whereupon he beat her. Then came, gorgeously dressed, the Council of State, who drank tea from tiny cups with his Majesty. But something went amiss, for the Queen enlisted their services in her favour, and they pulled the Emperor about the stage by his hind legs. Then he sang a comic song, and the mandarins played at leapfrog.

The play was followed by a tumbling performance, in which the chief feat of the tumblers was to jump off two tables, set one upon another, and fall flat upon their backs with a thud which ought to have broken their ribs. But they got up and did it again.

The whole business was a caricature of a pantomime, in which all in turn were clowns and pantaloons. The audience appeared to be gratified, for they laughed much. The price for the whole theatre, exclusive of two boxes tenanted by Chinese aristocrats, was the same—half a dollar, and barbarous music was kept up throughout the performance.

The Chinese are making progress here. They have built the Central Pacific Railway, but they do more than supply hands for hard work. There are wealthy mercantile houses owned and carried on by Chinese merchants. You not only see the humble laundry of Ho Ki, where the proprieter himself, in spectacles and pigtail, is patiently ironing a shirt by the window, but large wholesale establishments and offices with " Ho Sing, Wo Chung & Co." announced over the doors. They are fighting Californians with their own weapons and on their own ground ; and they are making such way that a popular comic placard in the town, representing the Irishman and the Chinaman with the head and boots of the American in their respective mouths, ends by picturing the Chinaman as having swallowed both Paddy and Uncle Sam. " Ah, sir," several persons said to me here, "the Chinese will soon reach New York, and presently you will see them in London." Their numbers do not increase very much, however, at present; but when once the China-man comes, not only with his gods and his theatre, but with his family, and gives up the sentiment which now makes him stipulate that his bones shall be re-stored to his own land, it is impossible to speculate on the Chinese flood which may pour into America.

No wonder an industrious, money-loving people like the Chinese admire California. This country, twice the size of Great Britain, possesses everything which makes a nation rich. Mountains and plains—the former covered with magnificent timber and filled with all mineral wealth, the latter deep with fertile soil, sea-board rivers, a most genial climate, and a position commanding the American and Eastern continents—make California the pregnant terminus of the first Atlantic and Pacific Railway. Great as has been its growth, it is still in its infancy. The consciousness of having unbounded opportunities gives the Cali-fornian an appetite for progressive change so great, and a craving for a fiercer speed so keen, that a native said to me one day, "We enjoy earthquakes." This, of course, is not true, but the sentiment is suggestive. Earthquakes are the flies in the ointment here. People were then looking out for one, as the weather had been peculiarly oppressive; and I saw many handsome houses being built of wood, as least likely to be thrown down. A gentleman resident there came into my room while I was writing, and told me the street talk was then of earthquakes. You heard the word from groups at the corners. He said "Last October travellers would not come into this hotel for a month." As I inhabited an apartment in the top story, I expected to have the sensation at its height if it had come.

Besides earthquakes, San Francisco is very apprehensive of fire, and the arrangements for the assemblage of engines (steamers), and notice to the inhabitants, are excellent. As elsewhere in America, the city is divided into wards, and its parts are numbered, the San Franciscan pocket-books having the numbers in them. Frequent telegraph signals communicate with a central building, which has a large bell. I have already referred to the procedure in case of fire. Suppose I live near telegraph station No. 56, and my house catches fire, I give a signal at once. The big bell tolls five times quickly, and then after a pause six times. The firemen all know where to go, and people in the street turn to their pocket-books to see where the fire has broken out. This tocsin is repeated to make the warning sure. It rang sometimes twice a night.

An industrial exhibition was open while I was there, and set forth well the resources of the country. I was struck by the abundance and apparent excellence of the machinery. The products, however, which first take the eye on a hot summer day are fruit and wine; the former is excellent and abundant. Strawberries are grown the whole year round; and the grapes, figs, pears, melons, limes, and peaches might make the mouth of a statue water. Melons are mostly eaten before breakfast. The waiter brings you one, say a foot and a half round, to begin with, as soon as you take your seat at the table. One morning I saw a gentleman break his fast with half a sphere which would have served for a dinner party of a dozen in London. I laid down my knife and fork to look at him, and he ate it up with a spoon. The other fare was good. Venison, and occasionally turtle, salmon, smelts, perch, cod, oysters, frogs, squirrels, quails, turkeys, beef, mutton, pork, &c.; with pastry and ice creams, Indian corn (of which the green ear is boiled whole, buttered and eaten as a dog gnaws a bone), sweet potatoes, huge tomatoes, and other vegetables, formed our ordinary dinner. Breakfast is similarly abundant, and lasts from 6 to 12. Luncheon comes on from 12.30, to 2.30, dinner from 4 to 7, tea from 7.30 to 9, supper from 9 to 12.

Though labour is dear here, food is not; the charge for daily board at this, which is one of the best hotels, being three dollars. Salaries are not bad, as the head waiter, who had been servant in a gentleman's family in England, told me he received eighty dollars a month, or about 240*l.* a year. But trifles are dear. "A bit," or 6*d.*, seemed the smallest current coin. You have a bottle, or rather glass, of soda water. "How much?" "A bit," and so on.

Education is made much of here. Some of the schools are very fine. I went over the Lincoln "grammar," or, as we should call it, "national" school, though the scholars remain longer than they do with us. It has more than 1,000 boys in attendance, and is divided into ten grades or standards, the lowest being the tenth. All but two are taught by mistresses. It is curious to see strapping young fellows of sixteen, with an incipient moustache, quietly obedient to a woman. The discipline is excellent. I never saw a school in better order. The writing of the tenth grade, where the children were six or seven years of age, was very good. The attainments of the scholars, so far as I could examine into them in two visits, were about equal to those of a very good national school in England. I asked one of the mistresses what work most of the children in her "grade" were intended for. "Work!" she replied, "we don't work here, we use our brains." The spelling was rather weak, the geography very fair, the arithmetic good and quickly done. More subjects, or at least, subjects with more names, were taught than with us. The first grade was having a lesson in "philosophy" while I was present. One boy was called upon to explain the construction of the kaleidoscope. Many common things were taught; but when I asked one of the elder scholars, a polite young man with a ring on his finger, whether they learnt "Euclid," he did not know what I meant. On my explaining the question, he said that geometry was taught in the High School. The boys were all bright, neat, and remarkably quiet. The frames of their slates were mostly covered with baize, lest they should rattle against the desks. I was kindly welcomed in the room of every grade, and the superintendent, who explained the processes of the school to mé, was most courteous. He said that in several respects he preferred the English system.

San Franciscans, in common with all Americans, are great readers, especially of newspapers. There are many of these, but the advertisements in some suggest great credulity on the part of the Californian public. The *Daily Call* is now open before me, and I see in one page seven advertisements of astrologers, one of which, as a specimen, announces that " Professor —— is the only practical planetary and electrical astrologer in the State. He can be consulted upon all sorts of business, law, robbery, sickness, love, or journeys by sea or land; fee, two dollars; by letter, three. Send the month of birth and year." Others profess " pure Arabian talismans for discovering rich mines." This does not indicate great progress in sound popular education.

San Francisco has many churches and chapels. I attended the service in six of them one Sunday. None were full. Nowhere, except in the Episcopal churches, was there any provision for kneeling, but the seats were all softly cushioned and very comfortable. A full-blooded negro conducted the evening service in the Baptist chapel. The congregation was very small, there being only about 42 people in the building, which would hold 500. But the preacher's language was superbly polysyllabic. An excellent sermon was being preached in one of the Presbyterian churches, which had the best congregation of all. Everywhere the proportion of men in the congregation was great. The Jews' synagogue is the most imposing religious edifice in the city, and the Roman Catholics have the largest number of adherents. I did not, however, visit any of their churches. In two of the churches, Baptist and Presbyterian, the congregation seemed to take no part whatever in the singing, but sat, the ladies all fanning themselves, and listened to a small choir, though hymns, not anthems, were sung, and the people held books in their hands. In both cases there was an organ. One Episcopal church had a surpliced choir, and full choral service.

Other public buildings are large, and have an air

of long-established success. Nothing, however, is more striking than the frequency with which you are reminded of the youth of the city. You may meet men in the prime of life who came here before the first house in San Francisco was built. And now it is a thriving city, and spreads like fire. One curious feature in its shifting growth is seen in the moving of whole houses down the streets from one part of the city to another. No wonder that the opening of the Atlantic and Pacific Railway has turned the eyes of America to this place, with its bay 50 or 60 miles long, and its varied incalculable possibilities of climate, position, and natural wealth. I met with very few travelling Englishmen while I was there. I searched the books of the Lick House and Occidental, leading hotels, to find in page after page no entry of an English arrival. The rush of visitors is American, and, as I conversed with many, I perceived that they came with a feeling that they were visiting almost another country. A gentleman said to me, "I can hardly believe that I am in America." The fame of California, however, is fast receiving a fresh impulse throughout the continent. There was during part of my visit a large party or deputation of "Odd Fellows" from all the States in the Union. They came in a special train, and the city newspapers were filled with accounts of the various sights and civilities which were shown to them by the authorities

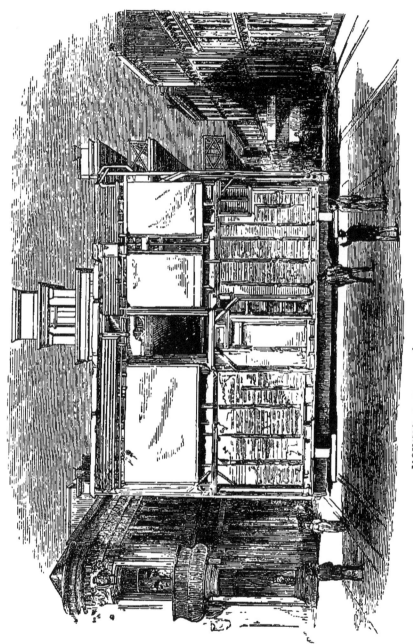

MOVING A HOUSE (FROM A PHOTOGRAPH).

G

of the place. Wherever you went you met a man with a ribbon in his button-hole, stating that he was member of such and such a Lodge in such and such a State. These gentlemen all seemed portly, prosperous, and full of the impressions which they were soon to take back to their own homes.

I have no space to tell you of the various excursions to be made in the beautiful bay of San Francisco. Its suburbs are stretching out miles away. I steamed and drove east and west, and the number of villas, &c., with wide gardens already occupied by men of business there was surprising.

The drive which pleased me most was that to the beach by the Cliffe House, about six miles off. I shall not soon forget my first sight of the shore of the Pacific. An American gentleman drove me in a "spider waggon," or "buggy," as it is called here, for miles along the beach. Our sharp wheels hardly made a track.

I never saw waves more translucent. The light shone through them till they broke with a pale emerald crest upon the clean hard sand. The sun set in the Pacific with a curious refraction which made it appear double, and then floods of purple, copper, and orange light were poured upon the sea and shore, which made the scene marvellously beautiful for a few minutes. Its strangeness was heightened to me by scores of seals, which were barking like Newfoundland dogs on the rocks, and strings of pelicans, which flew heavily over the waves.

From San Francisco I took one of the "excursions" of the place, to the Yo Semite Valley and the big trees. This impressed me again with the size of the country I was visiting. Everything is on a large scale. The route we followed was 250 miles in length, and it took twice as long to get into the beauties of the valley as it does to reach Switzerland from London.

CHAPTER VII.

· THE YO SEMITE VALLEY.

WE left San Francisco on a Tuesday afternoon, and reached the bottom of the Yo Semite Valley at 3.40 P.M. on a Friday, getting to the first house (there are only two) at 5.20. We took the Mariposa route, which is a little the longest, but passes through the finest scenery. It also enables the tourist to visit the largest group of big trees, which lie about five miles off the road. We had not seen them then, for we made the journey as fast as it could be conveniently accomplished. Indeed, a party which started from San Francisco a day before us, and which turned aside to visit the big trees, did not arrive till many hours after us.

Now for the route. We left San Francisco on Tuesday, at 4 P.M., in the Stockton boat, my companion being a very agreeable American gentleman, whom I will call G. There was a most glorious sunset on the bay, the mountains around which seemed to take every shade of violet, purple, and orange : passing divers steamboats propelled by one huge hind wheel, and watching the heavy flight of pelicans which abound here, we soon reached night. In the absence of the moon, the stars showed the river sides, and the lights of Benicia indicated the whereabouts of that pugilistic city. We met two or three monstrous hotel steamers, each of which looked like the side of a street afloat as they went by us with lamps shining from their tiers of windows. At last we turned in and woke the next morning at five to find our boat along-side the pier at Stockton, and one of the American " stages," with six horses, waiting to carry us on towards Mariposa. These vehicles are something like overgrown stage coaches, carrying nine inside and as many outside as can be piled upon the roof. Including the driver, our load was twenty-five. We started at six in the morning, and reached Hornitos, where the stage sleeps, at 8.30 P.M., the distance being 72 miles. The road—no, there was no road—the track lay across the dustiest flat ground I ever saw in my life. We made as much dust as half a dozen harrows on a dry ploughed field in August, and, as we went with the wind, we carried the dust with us all the way. Sometimes, while sitting outside, I could not see the leading horses—I mean that I could not have told whether we had leaders or not. The driver's face was as dirty as a clod of earth—nay, dirtier, for the dust had grown upon it like a fungus ; and when I washed mine in a tin basin before dinner at noon the water instantly became the colour of pea-soup. I never saw or heard of such dust.

In our case, however, the dust was mixed with a great store of oaths. The driver and his companion, who sat immediately before me, while I was outside, swore with an ingenious fertility of expletive discourse, which became at last as artistic as it was unpleasant. The way in which, when the main stream of decorated conversation flagged, they popped in little fragments of a curse just big enough to fill up a gap, showed the proficiency in swearing which must have been the result of long and skilful practice. I am bound to say that this performance was confined to a duet, the rest of the passengers being decent enough. One of them, however, was an example of the curious mixture which may be found in some of these Western parts. He sat opposite to me at dinner and ate like a hog. While his mouth was full he helped himself with his own knife and fork from all the dishes within his reach, placing food upon his plate in total disregard to the usual sequence or connection of courses. His hands were as dirty as—yes—as a scavenger's. Irish stew and apple pie, plum cake and pickles, mutton chops and cheese, all came and went together. When we were summoned to the stage, he sighed, and said, "That, sir, is a good square meal." And this trencherman turned out to be remarkably well informed and well behaved in conversation. I sat next to him after dinner, and listened to an argument he had with a fellow-passenger on the comparative advantages of a paper and specie circulation. He astonished me by his choice of words, their abundance, and the precision with which they were used. He spoke, too, with that slow, deliberate articulation and careful completion of every sentence which often marks the roughest-looking of some of these Western men. He talked as a prosperous man with plenty of money in his purse.

The scenery on this part of our route was dull enough. Right and left lay boundless breadths of corn-land, in which the large waggons, called here "prairie schooners," drawn by twelve horses, showed like ships. One farm we passed through consisted of 10,000 acres: the owner of this, a Mr. John Jones, letting in addition to tenants, who pay in kind, some 12,000 acres more. Some few years ago he had only fifty-three dollars and two yoke of cattle.

We passed large flocks of sheep, which are watched not only by shepherds but by turkey-buzzards, who, when a sheep drops, appear out of space and eat him. There were, besides, countless ground-squirrels, who live in harmony with little owls, many of which we saw sitting on their common mounds. There were no villages or towns in sight all day. We changed horses and dined at solitary ranches, one of which, "Bean Ranche," took its name from a habit which its owner once had of charging two dollars a head for dinner and giving his guests nothing but beans. We did not stop there, but dined excellently in the middle of the day at a place close to the Tuolumne river, which has the colour of carrot soup. This we crossed by a ferry, as we did two or three other streams. When we reached Hornitos at 8.30 we were so weary of the stage and unwilling to face the dust for five hours the next morning that we engaged a carriage, and, after a hasty supper, drove on to Mariposa, a place of much the same size as Hornitos, with a population of about 300 souls. We were very glad to get out of the stage, which, beside the dust it raised, showed a constant disposition to turn over, the road itself being exceeded in badness by its holes. In some places and for some distance this was mended with straw, as if the country side had been ill; but, mostly, the holes were left to grow as they liked, and when they were hopelessly impassable the stage took a turn into the field to avoid them.

We reached Mariposa at 2.15 A.M. on Thursday morning. There was one building with lights in the windows. "Is that the inn?" asked I of our driver. "No, sir," he replied, "it is a saloon. They are playing cards." However, we found the inn, with the door open. Entering, we shouted till somebody came and showed us our rooms, when we were asleep in five minutes.

Rising at about seven, we first visited the gold mine of Mariposa, and a civil Cornish miner gave me some quartz which contained gold at the rate of 200 dollars a ton. But some is very much richer. There is little "placer," or surface-digging, now. Most of the mines are worked by companies, and the quartz crushed at considerable expense. Here we saw the quartz reduced to white powder, then silted over copper plates smeared with quicksilver. The gold-dust unites itself with this. The amalgam is then scraped off and squeezed in a cloth till the quicksilver is pressed out, and a lump, from which the gold is finally extracted, left in the hands of the operator. Outside Mariposa we rode up to a party of Chinese surface diggers, and rashly proposed to buy what gold they had got. Fo, Fi, Fum & Co. rested on their spades and looked sadly at us till an interpreter came forward and conveyed to them the meaning of our pantomimic offers. They then shook their heads and went on patiently digging. They had found nothing but exercise in their labours, but had cast up a pyramid of dirt some twenty feet high.

After visiting the quartz mines we hired horses and a guide for an excursion to the Yo Semite, which takes a week at the least. Our guide was a very well-mannered young fellow, who took his meals with us on the route, and proved himself an excellent shot with a revolver. Our horses were hardy, sagacious greys, fitted with Mexican saddles. These are very uncomfortable at first, as you are obliged to ride with a long stirrup, and sit without varying your position in what might be the fork of a tree, the pommel rising in a way that would be more than disagreeable if the horse were to rear.

We had a ride of two long days through a forest which we entered shortly after leaving Mariposa. We reached a house called White and Hatch's about noon the first day. From that to the Yo Semite Valley we saw but one ranche—" Clark's "—where we slept. During the whole of the second day we met only one man, and he was on horseback, with a heavy rifle, hunting grizzly bears. We saw another man some little way off, building another ranche, which would probably be ready for tourists next year. Near Clark's, too, there were some wigwams of digger Indians, who had wonderful mops of coal-black hair on their shoulders, and earn a trifle by selling fish and other game. But they are a miserable race, eating, they say, not only acorns, but worms. Small parties, remnants of tribes, are scattered about these ridges of the Sierra Nevada, and exhibit the worst phases of a degraded disappearance. Squaws wandered about in front of me as I sat writing at the door of the ranche in the valley, and we tried to coax some round-headed, black-haired, staring brats, but they would have none of us, and ran away.

To return to our ride. It was unlike anything I
had ever experienced. The trail was "blazed"—*i.e.*,
marked by cuttings in the bark of trees. We wound
round mountain sides, and crawled up and down slopes
which tried the sureness of our horses' feet, as at last
they had to pass in the dark among stones and pieces
of rock lying in a trail which sometimes seemed as if
inclined at an angle of forty-five degrees, though,
of course, the descent was nowhere so steep. The
character of the scenery was unlike anything in Switzerland or the Tyrol, the mountains in one or other of
which countries I have visited for several summers.
It was, I think, chiefly marked by the absence of
underwood and the great size of the trees, chiefly pines,
cedars, and firs, which frequently rose as straight as
a stick without any indication of roots, out of a white
sandy soil. A very large number of the trees were
between 200 and 300 feet high. G. and I calculated
by means of its shadow the altitude of a tree sixteen
feet in circumference four feet six inches from the
ground, which stood a few yards from the door of our
ranche. I made it 204 feet high; he made it the
same all but a few inches. The height given by professor Whitney, one of the State Commissioners in
charge of this and the Mariposa tract, is, we learnt
from the keeper of the ranche, 208 feet. Now, this is
by no means an exceptional tree. Many among those
through which we wound our way as we rode were

much higher.   I believe that this proportion of large trees is caused by fires which fail to destroy those which have attained a considerable growth.   We saw many big trees flourishing with scorched trunks.   One very dark evening we had a fine scene presented to us. The night came on before we got to the place where we slept, and a portion of the forest on our left was in flames.   It was a grand, solemn sight.   Trees 100 feet high or more made pillars of fire which pointed up into a red sky.   On our right and in front the darkness was great.   I could sometimes see the grey horse of our guide when he was close before me.   Then for a few minutes I could perceive nothing but the outline of some of the tree tops against the starlight.   I hung my reins on the pommel of my saddle, and let my horse suit himself, which he did admirably, though sometimes his heels appeared to be higher than his head.   When we got near our ranche we fired our pistols as a signal, and our guide, reaching the flat in which the house lay, broke into a hand gallop, and took us in with great effect, though I, for one, could not see the ground over which we were passing.

That was on our reaching Clark's ranche.   The next day we rode still from 7 A.M. till 5.20, including stoppages for rest; but, as I said, we passed no house and met only one man—a bear hunter.   The scenery was much the same—with the exception of some sandy openings in the forest, which we cantered briskly over, and a few meadows of coarse grass, set round with high, straight cedar and pine trunks—till we reached Inspiration Point, at 12.40, where the first view is got of the Yo Semite Valley. I was disappointed. The prospect was obscured by smoke from a burning portion of the forest, and the sky-line of the mountains was more uniform than I had expected. We looked down into a narrow valley thick set with trees between nearly perpendicular cliffs 3,000 feet high. The view was not nearly so fine as many in Switzerland, though I do not remember any place surrounded by such precipitous rocks. These are of white granite. One which faced us as we descended by a very steep, rough, and dusty track presented what appears to be a perfectly unbroken perpendicular wall of 3,000 feet. There was no snow left, but the sky-line was jagged with scattered pines. It was not till we had fairly descended into the valley that we appreciated the singular feature of the scenery of the Yo Semite. The height of the trees conceals the slope of rubbish at the bottom of the cliffs, and thus they seem to rise sheer out of the ground like the sides of a house. A thin purple haze gave such a softness to the view that it was hard to believe we were looking upon the face of granite. The special beauty of the Yo Semite valley must be sought for in the spring, or at least early in the summer. The waterfalls, for which it is famous, are to be seen in their perfection only while the snow is melting. The Yo Semite Fall has, when it exists in perfection, one clear plunge of 1,600 feet. This is the highest, several of the others being repeatedly broken by ledges of rock. Some of the cascades were dry or reduced to a mere mockery of a dribble for some time, and would not reappear till the November rains gave them some substance. Their full beauty, however, is reserved for the spring thaw. Then, too, the valley is thick set with flowers. In summer it is dusty, and what grass there is is burnt brown. Still, the view of the granite cliffs over the green pine tops is always grand, and more continuously precipitous than any that I have ever seen. The valley is about seven miles long. There are in it two hotels, as they call themselves, but the accommodation is very rough. When G. and I were shown to our bedroom the first night we found that it consisted of a quarter of a shed screened off by split planks, which rose about eight or ten feet from the ground, and enabled us to hear everything that went on in the other "rooms," which were simply stalls in the same shed. Ours had no window, but we could see the stars through the roof. The door, opening out into the forest, was fastened with cow-hinges of skin with the hair on, and a little leather strap which hooked on to a nail. We boasted a rough, gaping floor, but several of the other bed-rooms were only strewed with branches of arbor vitæ. As a grizzly bear had lately been seen wandering about a few hundred yards from our "hotel," we took the precaution of putting our revolvers under our pillows. I dare say this was needless, as the bears have mostly retired to the upper part of the valley, a few miles off, but it gave a finish to our toilet which had the charm of novelty. Next morning, however, seeing the keeper of the ranche with his six-shooter in his hand, and noticing that it was heavily loaded, I asked him why he used so much powder. "Oh," said he, "I've loaded it for bears."

At first G. and I were the only visitors at this house, but several were at the other one about half a mile off, and more were soon expected. Altogether some 800 persons visited the valley this year. Out of the 368 whose names were entered in the book here I found those of only three English people and one Scotchman. The number of tourists had largely increased that summer, but I do not think very many will come till a railroad has been made to Mariposa from Stockton, and the discomfiture of the middle passage over the dusty plains thus obviated.

There are, as I have said, a few Indians in the valley, but they belong to the Mono Tribe, which has driven out that of the Yo Semite. Indeed, only one man of these was left, and he expected to be shot before long, for the remnants of these miserable

tribes were still at war with each other. The last of
the Yo Semite Indians had fled from the home of his
ancestors, and lived with three squaws in a bark
wigwam close to Clark's ranche, where we slept on
our way. We saw him as we passed. Those then
there were, I believe, Monoes. Not far off from the
"hotel," the squaws I saw were pounding acorns for
their winter food, two or three of their lords and
masters looking on. We paid them a visit during the
course of our sojourn in the valley, and they scowled
at us horribly. No wonder, poor wretches; for
though they turned out the Yo Semite tribe, they are
themselves finally disappearing before the white man,
who has come into this, which was to the Indians one
of their most famous retreats. Some few years ago
the Yo Semite natives killed several of a party of
miners, and then were foolish enough to boast that
they lived in a valley safe from the white man; but a
traitor of another tribe took the avengers into this
place. I had the honour of being introduced to him
on my way there, but did not know then that he had
played the Judas to the redfaces. I met him in the
forest. He was riding, while three of his ladies were
toiling alongside on foot, through the deep dust, with
heavy burdens on their backs. It seems that I
resemble some officer of weight and size whom he
once honoured. "Whew! whew!" whistled he as I
rode past. "Who this?" he then asked of our

guide. "Great Captain? whew! whew! Hew dew dew?" added he to your humble servant, stopping to shake hands. "Hew dew dew? Wheeew wheeeeew."

I add a few lines about the remainder of our visit to the valley, leaving that to the big trees for another chapter. During the three days we were there we wandered about and found the permanent features of the scenery grow upon us. The granite cliffs are wonderful. We looked in vain, though, for our grizzly bear. One night we thought we had perhaps found him. G. and I strolled out into the forest with our revolvers, and presently disturbed something which made a crackling and brushing in the long dry undergrowth, and seemed to go up a tree. It was too dark to see any object distinctly, for we had only starlight to guide us. So we fired up into the branches whence the noise came, but got only prolonged echoes among the cliffs for our pains. One of our visitors, though, came upon a lynx not far from our house, and several deer were killed and brought in by the Indians; and one man told us he had shot fifty-eight bears in the last four years.

There is but very little cultivation in the valley. One enterprising man had planted a spot with vegetables, and pear, apple, plum, and peach trees. Where he found a market for their produce it was hard to say, unless, as is probable, he relied upon selling to visitors what he could not eat. His orchard had no fence, and he himself was not to be found when we paid it a visit. Outside a little hut, however, close by, was a paper, with the following notice : " Any one helping himself to a mess of fruit from my patch will please put 2 Bits through a hole in my door, and oblige J. C. Lemon." We helped ourselves liberally to peaches and apples, and complied with his request, adding a little more for the pocketfuls we took away.

One day we climbed as far into the recess behind the Yo Semite falls as we could reach, and realised the great size of the cavity. The pleasure of strolling and sitting about in these parts is somewhat marred by rattlesnakes, whose trails are seen in the dust, and which you may find coiled up on a stone that seems to offer a pleasant seat. Nothing is now to be feared from the Indians, who were once the most dangerous inhabitants of the valley. There is, indeed, no serious reason why a peaceful traveller should carry firearms in these parts. We were tempted to bring ours for the possible chance of a shot at a lynx or a grizzly bear. In a few years the last of these will have retired before the stream of tourists. A railway will be built to the foot of the Sierra, a shorter trail made to the Yo Semite from Mariposa, and it will be difficult to realise the loneliness and roughness of our ride through the forest to this place. All the Americans I have seen are very proud of it, and some less well informed than the rest have been almost offended at my saying that much grander mountain views could be found in the Alps. I was far more impressed with the forest than with the valley, though I had not then seen the famous big trees.

CHAPTER VIII.

TO THE FOREST.

I HAVE just returned to Sacramento from our Yo Semite excursion. Though the valley has disappointed me, I am more than glad to have taken our forest ride and visited the big trees in the Mariposa district. They are monstrous. We left the valley on Monday morning at 7 A.M., riding to "Clark's" that day by the same route as the one followed on our entrance. The forest grew upon us. My companion said to me, "I seem never to have seen trees before," and yet those through which we rode were of no uncommon size for these parts. As we passed by one I said, "Now, that is not an exceptional tree; let us measure it." So we got off our horses, and, taking out my tape, I found it was, breast high, 18½ feet in circumference. The trunks of many pines, too, run up far as clean as a mast. The sun striking on these, which are of a light yellowish brown colour, and on those of the cedars, which are very large, clean, and reddish, gives marvellous vistas in the forest. Some trees are also loaded with bright green moss, and as the *arbor vitæ* reaches a great height—say, 50 feet or 60 feet—its dark foliage adds to the play of colour which surrounds the traveller in these immense belts of timber. Large fallen rotten trunks and charred stumps are seen in all directions, and the sentiment of loneliness is increased by the thought that one might ride a thousand miles through the same scenes by following the course of the Sierra. But the grandest of all are, I think, reserved for the night. We had eaten our supper at Clark's ranche, and I was sitting within doors by a roaring log fire smoking my cigar, for it was cold, when G. called to me to come out. Part of the mountain which we had been descending for hours, and which, covered with huge trees, rose high up from our resting-place, was on fire. We had been aware of much smoke during the day, but our track had not led us near the scene of the conflagration. The sight was infinitely grand. High up, as it were, in the sky, we saw walls, towers, and pinnacles of fire. In some places it smouldered in long banks and lines of glowing red, and then arose in crackling pillars of flame, as some great tree broke into a blaze. Here and there huge ladders of light seemed to reach up to the fiery firmament from the earth. The shifting of the flashes, as a trunk fell or some fresh branches were caught, gave an appearance as if some monster forms were moving about in the middle of the furnace. We stood long in silence looking at it. The fire was not very far off, perhaps two hours' ride, and reached only for some few miles. It had been burning for a month. The way in which it was piled upon itself, and had crept up the mountain side, leaving great trunks to smoulder and glare for weeks beneath its course, gave it a perspective like that of Martin's pictures. We said it was worth coming to the Yo Semite if it were only to behold such a scene as that. Altogether, what with the burning forest, the bark wigwams by which we stood, and the roaring log fire outside the ranche, around which rough men sat as if in a picture of Rembrandt, that evening was one of the most marked in our ten days' excursion to the valley.

A word about Mr. Clark before I pass on. I suppose he might be called a pioneer of settlers and back-woodsmen. One of his dependants told me that he frequently preferred a blanket by the wood fire under the stars to a bed in the house which is known by his name hard by. To look at him, with his rough dress, rougher beard, and trousers, Western fashion, stuck into his boots, you might carelessly put him down for a coarse, tobacco-chewing, swearing son of the forest. But take a flower or a fir cone in your hand and ask him what it is. He will give you at once its Latin name in soft measured speech and with courteous rejoinder. He had a few books in the window of the ranche. I laid my hand at once on Göthe's "Faust" and Robertson's Sermons. Again and again we met with combinations or contrasts of character in the same individual which, I think, could hardly be found in the Old World. Here, if anywhere, is the place to learn that people are not always what they seem. The exigencies of border life involve the roughest outside and the hardest hand; but, at the same time, they weed out those who have nothing but bone and sinew to help them. A pioneer must not only have a thick skull, but keen brains inside it. Moreover, the love of adventure and the sense of battle done with mine, forest, and plain, let alone Indians and "grizzlies," have drawn divers men of good education and prophetic soul out of smoothed civilised society, where they fretted at small proprieties, and they rejoice at having full fling for their wits and limbs by laying down a way for their nation to follow into the incalculable stores of a new world.

Next morning we started shortly after sunrise for the big trees. It was very cold, and we enjoyed the gallop which a comparatively level track gave us through the first part of the forest which we entered. Soon our path grew too steep for more than a footpace. We went up and down among the trees for about two hours, until our guide cried out, "We shall come to one directly;" and sure enough there stood a red-barked monster, dwarfing the large trunks among which it grew, as a full-grown tree does a crowd of saplings. Where were our pines, with their 18 feet girth, by the side of a giant some 100 feet round breast high? Of course the great size of the ordinary forest timber in which these huge growths are found takes off from their immense proportions, but if one were set upon a plain it would show like the Eddystone Lighthouse. To speak for myself, it was hard to realise that what we saw were trees. Their trunks, when we stood close to them, had almost the appearance of artificial structures. One that had fallen was hollow, and had been broken by its fall. We rode into the break and through the prostrate fragment as if it had been a tunnel. We climbed up on the trunk of another, also fallen, and when I had stepped 55 yards upon it I measured its circumference and found it to be over 25 feet. Thus, with its bark on—it had been stripped—it would have been at least some 30 feet in girth at a height of 170 feet from the ground. But these were not the biggest that we saw.

The bark of these trees is red, and about a foot thick. It lies on the trunk in rough longitudinal ridges like huge muscles, but it is so soft that with my pocket knife I cut off two great hunks from a portion which had been detached, and lay upon the ground. The branches are short, and spring mainly from the upper part of the tree. The foliage is scant

STUMP OF A BIG TREE (FROM A PHOTOGRAPH).

in proportion to the trunk, and the cones are little bigger than plovers' eggs. The tree itself is said to be a species of gigantic cedar; but it spends its strength in growing more wood than leaves. There are about 600 of these cedars, of different sizes, some being comparatively small, in the Mariposa groups. I do not know the greatest height reached by any one of these, but in another grove the altitude of one is found to be 335 feet, and there also a fallen hollow trunk can be ridden through on horseback for a distance of 25 yards. One fallen tree is said to measure upwards of 420 feet, but I doubt this. The Mariposa group is not so well known as several others, and consequently has not suffered from the enterprise of some shrewd settler in these parts who profanes the scene with a catchpenny " hotel," like a " camera obscura" on the beach at Margate. I see by photographs that several giant trees have these parasites at their feet. Here we met with no such offence, but rode about from trunk to trunk by a trail which was occasionally almost lost and sometimes left. The fancy of visitors has been to give names to the largest. " This," said our guide, " is 'Grant;' this is 'Johnson,' because it leans to the South," and so on. But the trees themselves were not thus labelled, and in spite of this prattle, which could not be stopped, we carried away a deep impression of these wonderful growths.

After spending as long a time as we could spare in visiting and measuring this group, we rode back to Clark's, as we had to push on that afternoon to "White and Hatch's," the next house on the way towards Mariposa. I had made such a collection of pieces of wood, bark, cones, &c., that it had to be packed up before and behind me when I got into the saddle. This made our progress slow, for it is not easy to trot or gallop with a woodstack around you, and the night came on before we got to our quarters.

Next night we rode into Mariposa betimes to catch the stage for Stockton; and I hope, for the sake of any future visitors to the district, that this may be superseded by a railway before long. I never in my life heard of any one who had gone through the jolting which we were condemned to for five hours. The stage had no springs, and the road, "graded," or roughly cut on the sides of the spurs of the Sierra, had not been made. I dare say it never will be, for when an American has got so far with a track as to make it just passable for wheels he is content. Our route looked at a distance as good as that over any of the lower Swiss passes; but, since the floor of the rock which had been laid bare for it by pick or blast was simply left to level itself, the result was merely a rough sketch of a road. There were eight of us in the stage, which had a leathern roof supported by strong uprights. We all held on by these, or we should have been a mere conglomerate of travellers before the journey ended. Up-hill it was not so bad, for we went very slowly; but when our driver had reached the top of the zigzags which lead down to Hornitos he drove as fast, I suppose, as he could, and the result inside was ludicrously disagreeable. At Hornitos we had to wait some six hours for the next start of the stage; only now it was a "Concord" coach with six horses, nine inside passengers, and any number out. Here the jolting and bad management were in some respects worse, for they became dangerous. Our driver had provided himself with a store of whisky, which he soon drank. Then an outside passenger was foolish enough to give him a flask full in addition. The result was that he drove off the track into the country. Now, as this happened in the middle of a dark, moonless night, and as the country consisted of rounded hills, with occasional watercourses, the *détour* was not agreeable. It was so dark that even our tipsy driver was compelled to stop two or three times and get down to the ground to search for wheel marks or any indication of a road. At last we struck the track, and away he went with his six horses as hard as he could pelt. There was nothing to be done. We were wedged in so tight that we could not move or even jolt about inside, but the lumbering vehicle bounded along as if it were as drunk as the coachman. By all the rules of dynamics we ought to have been turned over half-a-dozen times. One provoking feature of the performance was the praise which a fellow-Irishman bestowed on the driver for not upsetting us when he left the road.

The scenery through which the traveller passes on his way to the forest on the sides of the Sierra is not pleasing. It reminded me of the least agreeable phases of a summer Italian prospect. The grass was burnt brown, and the short stunted oaks had the roundness and monotony of olive trees. I can well imagine that the spring here is lovely, but six months' roasting sun so pulverises the soil that it becomes coated, not with sand, but with the finest powder, which rises in clouds round every footfall, and, once raised, shows no more disposition to settle down again than smoke does. It obscures the horizon, and dims the outline of even near objects with a choking yellow haze. And yet this dun-coloured soil becomes almost black when irrigated. One spot by the road-side was cheered by a Chinaman's garden. He had brought a little stream to his aid, and his cabbages stood up as clean and bright out of the dark mould as they do in a Chinese picture. The neatness and regularity of this plot were all the more striking as our way along ran by the side of deserted surface gold mines. Nothing can exceed the desolate look of these. It seemed as if those who had dug had been so fierce for gain as to dig wildly. No vestige of order or method survived. The object of the miners was to wash every likely spot along the valley, and as they came upon a good "find," to turn up every foot around it, greedily careless about leaving their work as ragged as possible. Their "tailings" had been picked over by successors, often with as much success as some of the first eager diggers met with; and now patient Chinese were to be seen in places turning over and "washing" the tormented earth for such gleanings of gold as it still contained. But each generation of miners has made the scene more scraggy and desolate. The poor valley has no sooner begun to clothe some of its sores with vegetation than they are rudely scratched open again.

As I said, however, this "placer" mining has mostly been superseded by the quartz mill, which is fed from the shaft. The true surface mines of California are its corn-fields, gardens, and vineyards. I have already referred to these, but I do not think that I mentioned one "garden" which has forty acres of strawberries. Judicious irrigation, in a climate which really has no winter, enables this fruit to be provided the whole year round.

Before I close this chapter I must say something about the cost of a trip to the Yo Semite. The

A SURFACE GOLD MINE, PARTLY WORKED OUT (FROM A PHOTOGRAPH).

barest expenses for the excursion from San Francisco
amount to more than 100 dollars, gold. The charge
for living on the route and in the valley is exorbi-
tant. We paid three dollars and a-half each per day
for the sorriest lodging and the simplest fare. We
had, moreover, to pay the same for our guide, in
addition to his own wage. Then extras were charged.
The toll over a rude bridge was one dollar a horse.
Altogether the visitor must expect to be squeezed as
dry as possible. Probably competition will change
this before long; but at present all concerned in exhibiting the Yo Semite combine to get as much as
they can out of the sight-seer. You are obliged to
ride, at least in the summer and autumn. Dust
would make a walking tour there intolerable. As it
is, the inside of the legs of your trousers become like
that of an old flower-pot. Almost all who live there
wear high boots, with their trousers stuck in them.
This is by far the best foot gear for these parts.
But, however shod, no one walks. You must have
a horse for your guide, for which you pay extra; and
if you have anything like luggage, you must have a
horse for that too.

Of course, if any one were to make a lengthened
tour or sojourn in and about the Sierra, he would
take his tent and camp out, but now ordinary tourists
or travellers have no choice but to submit to extor-
tion or keep clear of the Yo Semite.

I ought to add that we found the people we had to do with civil; our guide especially was a very well-behaved young fellow. We were charged high for almost everything, but there was no help for it, and if one is squeezed, it is as well to be squeezed as pleasantly as possible.

CHAPTER IX.

THE MORMON CITY.

My return journey eastward from California was broken by a visit to the Salt Lake City, and as by the failure of the Union Pacific Railway to keep its time I was obliged to wait at Omaha for a night, I took the opportunity of putting down on paper something about the Mormons.

I cannot affect to arrange my impressions in a manner which shall give you distinct tabulated information under such different heads as politics, religion, agriculture, and the like—I can best set down what comes uppermost in what I saw and heard during an eight days' sojourn in the City of the Saints.

The Atlantic and Pacific Railway, though it skirts the Great Salt Lake, nowhere runs within thirty-five miles of the Salt Lake City. A coach took you to it by an abominable road from Uintah. A branch railway, however, was opened not long after my visit, and now the seclusion of Brigham Young's famous town has been impaired for ever. Some Mormons affected to be pleased with the prospect of this publicity, but I didn't believe them. Certainly, no sign of a desire to be visited was then shown by their authorities, if we may judge by the state of the road which led to the city from the Uintah Station. It is more full of deep holes than any I ever traversed. Two stages ran daily—one meeting the eastward and the other the westward train; but the influx of strangers by these was inconsiderable in a city of some 20,000 inhabitants. Since the branch railway has been opened, hundreds have been tempted to have a passing look at the City of the Saints, where one submitted to the long jolting imposed once upon visitors. There seems no reason, moreover, why, having once been invaded by the rail, the Mormons should not see it carried by the Valley of the Jordan and the Utah Lake through their country settlements. However their rulers may wish to remain isolated, the people will see the superiority of a train to the old tedious waggon, and will probably prefer being hanged for a sheep rather than for a lamb. The deed is done. The iron road has bored its way through the shell of Mormonism, and the Saints must make the best of it. Rumour says that Brigham has already made a very good thing of it indeed, as he took the contract for many miles of the Union Pacific.

We left Uintah Station at about noon, the train steaming off on its single line of rail for its solitary

journey over the wilderness. Having secured two
seats outside the stage, we looked with special interest
on our route and its surroundings. The road ran at
the foot of hills on our left. On our right lay a flat
country dotted with Mormon farms; beyond it the
beautiful Salt Lake twinkled in the sun; and across
this, some forty miles off, rose a grand range of snow-
patched mountains.

.We met a large number—almost a procession—of
tilted carts, each driven by an elderly, shaven, sour-
faced man. In the carts were beds, kettles, baskets,
&c., among which sat one or more of the sour-faced
men's wives. Not to mince the matter, I never saw
such a collection of ugly, shrivelled, melancholy-
looking women in my life. They wore long poke
bonnets, like the tilted carts they rode in, from under
tho roofs of which they scowled at the stage as their
lords and masters drew on one side to let us pass.
We learnt from our driver, a surly fellow, that they
were leaving the half-yearly conference, which had
just broken up, and that some of them had come 200
or 300 miles to attend it. Hence the beds, kettles,
&c. At first we were sorry to have missed this
gathering, but perhaps it was for the best, as we
came upon much sentiment which the conference had
just aroused.

The scene remained the same for several hours.
At last, on reaching the top of a rise in our road,

THE TABERNACLE, SALT LAKE CITY (FROM A PHOTOGRAPH).

we saw sloping gently from the hill on our left
what appeared to be a long shrubbery, thick-set
with gables, walls, and chimneys, and in the midst of
it a huge white oval rounded roof, like a monstrous
egg.   This was the City of the Saints, and the egg
was the Tabernacle.   We soon entered the town.
Each house, as a rule, stands in an orchard of small
trees.   The streets are very wide, unlighted, unpaved,
and skirted on either side by small streams of water.
They are, as is usual in American towns, at right
angles to each other, and on three sides—the slope of
the hills prevents the streets going far on the fourth
side—stretch out towards the plain ready for any
extension of the city, and pointing towards the still
unoccupied valley flats.   The extreme perspective of
these streets is very striking.   Shortly after we were
put down at the Townsend House, a hotel kept by a
man of that name and his three wives, I strolled into
the city. . As I stood looking down one of these wide
thoroughfares, I perceived a cloud of dust in the
distance, and waited to see what it would bring forth.
Presently horsemen became visible, and before long a
tribe of Indians revealed itself.   The chief rode first.
Then came a mixed multitude of warriors and
squaws, almost all riding, the latter astride like the
men, with children seated behind, holding on.   It
was a picturesque troop, but all were repulsively ugly.
They were moving camp, and had come into the town

to trade by the way. I saw in some shops stores of glass beads, which the saints, at a very considerable profit, used as precious coin in their transactions with these people. Among the things sold by the Indians are buffalo robes, admirably dressed by the squaws. As I bought one for six dollars and a-half, and have no doubt the vendor did not lose by the sale, the Indians do not receive a very high price for their work.

But to return to the Mormons. I took every opportunity of conversing with them and seeing what was going on. We had the honour of an interview with Brigham Young. He sent word that he would be ready to see us at 10 A.M., two days after our arrival. Picture a broad, white, dusty road, lined with two rows of low trees, and a graystone wall on the left-hand side. Behind this lay Brigham's two houses, and the detached school-room which he has built for his many children. One house, the first as you approach, has the figure of a recumbent lion on the top. This is the Lion House. The next is crowned by a bee-hive. This is the Bee-hive House. The next, approached by an arch over which stands the large effigy of a bird with outspread wings, is the "Eagle," or school-house. We saw him in the Bee-hive. There are three doorways in the wall, from which a few steps lead to three separate entrances. One opens into the telegraph office—Saints must' send their messages through that; another into the reception-room of the President, as he is called. We entered by this, and found ourselves in a good-sized apartment, with brown sofas, a table with stereoscopic slides, &c., upon it, and pictures in oil of the twelve Apostles (Mormon) hung upon the walls. There were also a few photographs of some places on the Union Pacific, and a glaring advertisement of a steam fire-engine. The farther part of the room was shut off by a low screen with a glass top. Behind it, at the end, were oil paintings of Joseph and Hiram Smith, a clock, a few books of reference, and Brigham's desk, with a number of letters upon it waiting his arrival. His private secretary took our cards in, and presently the great man himself entered by a side door, and, shaking hands, begged us to be seated on a sofa, while he took a chair in front and conversed with us. He was dressed in a black frock-coat and trousers, with a white waistcoat. He is about five feet eight inches in height, thick-set, with whiskers of light brown hair meeting under his chin. He has small light-blue eyes, a slightly aquiline nose, a square business-like head, a tight-set mouth, and a strong jaw. I was much struck, however, with his jaded, weary look. They say he has aged much in the last six months, being now in his seventieth year. He evidently considered us bores, if not spies. We had some general conversation about Hepworth

Dixon's book, which he said he didn't like—the extension of the city, the Pacific Union Railway, and the advantages enjoyed by those who had emigrated to the Salt Lake, concerning which he asked me the names of some poor people whom I knew formerly in London, and said if they did right they would fare well. Then we made our bow, and went away, the President politely shaking hands with us again at our departure. Whilst there, I may remark that divers of his children were running about, and he took one pretty girl between his knees as he sat receiving us.

We saw him and a bevy of his wives another day at the theatre, where he has a rocking-chair to himself in the middle of the pit. He did not occupy it, however, on that occasion, but sat in the stage-box with a lady who they said was his favourite wife Amelia. Other wives, with a swarm of his children, sat elsewhere. There are twenty-three of the former living, beside a number to whom he is merely "sealed," and I believe about forty of the latter, mostly girls. I tried hard to get photographs of some of his wives, but, though they have been taken, they are forbidden to be sold. The theatre is large and badly lit. There is nothing in its arrangements to mark its difference from any other. It has a pit and three galleries, and looks very dirty. The pit is apparently appropriated by resident Mormon families. We saw divers men coming in with their three, four, or more wives. Nobody dresses for the performance, and there is a good deal of talking between whiles. The piece was "A New Way to Pay Old Debts." It was badly acted, but the audience laughed on small provocation, and seemed to enjoy itself. Gentiles and Mormons were present. Those sitting close by us in the front of the lower gallery were, I suppose, Gentiles. They seemed to know each other. A young man next me, levelling his opera-glass at Brigham when he entered his box, said to his companions, "Ah! there is the old devil; who has he got with him to-night? Oh, it's Amelia."

From what I saw and heard, I much doubt if Brigham's popularity among a minority of the Mormons is very strong. Lately Mormon workmen held mass-meetings to protest against his lowering their wages, and carried their point. I was credibly assured that he tried to take half-a-dollar off their daily pay. Moreover, Mormon labour is not paid fully in money. I asked divers working Saints what they got. "Well," they said, "we get—so much." "But do you see the money?" I inquired. "No, not all," they replied; "part is paid in orders on the stores." Thus they are tied by the tooth, and find it hard to get away, especially as when they receive notes they are of Salt Lake currency, useless beyond the territory. These, however, they can change for greenbacks, at least in small quantities. I am

STREET IN SALT LAKE CITY, AND THEATRE (FROM A PHOTOGRAPH).

convinced that many Mormons feel the pressure of their inquisitorial government more than they like to admit. They wriggle about under cross-questioning, and make a poor business of putting a good face on the matter. The city is divided into—I think it is twenty-one wards. Over each of these a Bishop presides. Thus a Bishop looks after about 1,000 people. He is aided by a number of teachers, who call upon each family once a-month and report on their conduct.

I give a specimen of the sort of conversation I had with Mormons in one that I held with a young man whom I knew in London, and who, indeed, with much expression of surprise at seeing me there, hailed me in the street. "Now," said I, "tell me what the teacher does." "Why, he comes in and we all sit round the room." "What does he do then?" "Well, he asks us questions." "Of what kind?" "Oh, whether we have attended to our prayers, paid our tithing, and been to meeting, and such like." "Anything else?" "Well, he will speak to us if the floor is not clean, and such like." "Can't you shut him out?" "Guess not." "What would happen if you declined to see him?" "Why, he would report us to the Bishop, and if we wouldn't let him in we should be cut off from the Church." "A man can't call his house his castle here, then?" He looked at me and shook his head.

This "cutting off from the Church" is a serious thing, for it means no work to be had of Mormons, no help, no charity, no pity. Curiously enough, I stumbled upon an old man who had been servant in the family of a great-aunt of mine. He had given up Mormonism, and found employment with the rector of the Episcopal mission here. I asked him how he had fared. He had been a devout Mormon, and was one of those who in former days had actually crossed the plains on foot, dragging a hand-truck with his goods and leading his wife. "Sir," he said, "I got on well for some time; then I left some of my flour behind me. Many died. I thought I should not mind lying down to die myself. I was wore out. Then I stopped at one of the places where the overland stage changed horses, and hired myself to cook for passengers. There was very good wages, for the cook was killed about every five months by the Indians; but somehow I got on well with the Indians. I stayed there till I had saved 800 dollars in gold. Then I started again for Salt Lake City and bought, as I thought, a lot of ground; but there worn't no written paper about it, so he took my money and I didn't get my lot. That worn't right, sir, so I guv it up."

Now this is a true story. Such things, of course, shake the confidence of some Mormons, and I was not surprised to hear many complaints; but the

chief source of possible division arises just now from
the two sons of Joseph Smith, David and Alexander,
who are lecturing against polygamy—*i.e.*, against
Brigham Young—in the Salt Lake City. We heard
them both, and had some private conversation with
Alexander. I will allude now, however, only to what
occurred in public. On Sunday afternoon I attended
the service in the Tabernacle, where I heard a violent
sermon by Mr. Smith, Brigham's first councillor,
mainly on the exclusiveness, isolation, or peculiar
sanctity of the Saints, and polygamy. First, he
praised Brigham Young. He reminded them of what
their President had done, and the persecutions
through which they had passed. He urged their
respect for him. This looked suspicious, for if the
congregation had heartily loved him they would not
have wanted such recommendations as I heard given.
They sounded like excuses rather than praise. Then
he went on to urge the necessity of separation and
the danger of Gentile influence. He rated them
soundly for the readiness with which some of them
followed Gentile fashions. Then he pressed upon
the people the holiness of polygamy. I sat facing
hundreds of melancholy-looking women, who occupied
the seats in the middle of the building, and narrowly
watched the array of sad faces to see if I could detect
a responsive glance. But there was none, though, as
I fancied, a look of deeper sadness came upon those

who were nearest to me. He thundered on about polygamy. He instanced, of course, Abraham, David, and Solomon—Mormons are rather shy of talking about Adam, who only had one Eve given to him— he assured them that the Fathers were divinely and specially right in having many wives; and, after declaring that unless polygamy were of God's appointment every Bible ought to be burnt, wound up by dragging in Christ among the supporters of that practice, and triumphantly concluded his sermon with the sentence from the Book of Revelation: "I am the root and offspring of David, the bright and morning star," as a characteristic saying of Jesus, who thus "nobly boasted of his descent from the great polygamist."

Full of this deliverance, I rushed off to the Independence Hall, where David and Alexander Smith were then holding forth. I found the place crowded with Mormons, and could not get a seat. David was preaching, and there was little in his sermon which differed much from what might be heard at a highly-spiced Methodist meeting. Then Alexander began the business of the afternoon. He showed that polygamy was forbidden by the Book of Mormon, which they had in their hands. He waxed warm. He cried, "Shame upon it, and upon the author (Brigham Young) of this confusion!" He called his teaching "foul, false, and corrupt." I had my note-book, and put down the words at the time. Nothing could exceed the plainness with which he denounced polygamy. The audience listened with the deepest interest. One Mormon standing by me muttered once, " That is a —— lie," though the Saints are specially prohibited from swearing.

I might mention that, in the conversation which we had afterwards with this Alexander Smith, he complained that Brigham had refused to lend him the Tabernacle—I didn't wonder at that—but had actually lent it, on the same day that he (Smith) had applied for it, to a sectarian minister—I think a Methodist. This shows that Smith thoroughly believes himself, and expects others to admit his claim, to be a pure Mormon. And thus, with the prestige which belongs to him as a son of the founder of the Mormon faith, he is a formidable opponent to the President. And, we may inquire, if polygamy goes, what will become of Mormonism ? I asked several Mormons, and they said it would perish. Others said it would not. One thing I was convinced of—many of the married women detest polygamy. Of course it is the interest of Brigham and his chiefs to urge men to take more than one wife. By doing this they are tied up; for if polygamy were discarded as an essential item in Mormon practice, the position of men with more wives than one would be very unpleasant, and the poor wives would find themselves worse than nowhere. But I doubt if polygamy grows. I asked divers Mormons who argued for it if they practised it themselves. "No," they said, "but we might if we chose, and we will if we like." To one or two I said, "Tut, tut, man; the reason is simply that you dare not. Your wife wouldn't let you." In mentioning this, I cannot help remarking the freedom with which Mormons now submit to Gentile criticisms. I ever spoke quite openly, drawing their attention to the mess into which the community was getting itself should the United States' Government interfere. Some scowled, some grinned. The Pacific Railroad has so impressed them with a sense that their fortifications have been carried, that, in the Salt Lake City at least, you may pick up a Mormon in the streets and get him theologically, socially, or politically into a hole, without, I suppose, much risk. Some time ago you would possibly have been shot. Now the Mormons are quarrelling among themselves, and are obliged to allow a certain expression of difference from strangers. One day while we were there a large party of Americans, excursionists by rail, came from Delaware. They stayed at our hotel. In the evening a zealous Mormon was tempted to try his tongue on this mass of Gentiles. He had one of the ante-rooms full to listen to him. A gentleman of the Delaware party, apparently a lawyer, sat down in a chair, and, cocking his legs up, laid a series of theological and social traps for this zealot, into which he made a number of dangerous falls.

The situation of the town is lovely. The industry of the people is commendable, though no better than that of many settlers, and not so great as that of the man who has to clear the soil from trees before he can plough his field. When I came to look into it, I found that the barrenness of the plain is exaggerated. There is abundance of excellent soil and water. I had occasion to go into the middle of the valley to look for flint implements in some old Indian mounds, and on my way passed through divers farms. The settler had simply to plough his lot and burn the sage-grass which grew upon it. Elsewhere I found good natural herbage, which the cattle were enjoying. Thus the Mormon farmer may thrive well, especially as he may take four or five extra wives, whom he sends out into the fields to work, and thus gets labour at small cost; but as for any special difficulties which he encounters in settling himself when once in the valley, I do not believe in them. The soil grows everything. Perhaps the chief natural drawback to farming here arises from the number of insects. The breaking up of the land, however, and the planting of trees, will probably bring more small birds, which will tend to set the balance straight. The valley produces cotton, sugar-cane—I saw them crushing the canes—silk, besides all kinds of fruit and corn. This is inconsistent with what we have heard about the place being naturally a wilderness. It has deep mould, a glorious sun, and fresh-water streams pouring into it from all sides, and is thus a very paradise for a settler as far as Nature is concerned.

But in this paradise is gathered the cream of European, specially British, fanaticism. None but those hungering after or weakly open to strongly sensational religious demands are likely to listen to Mormonism as a spiritual creed. How many embrace or adhere to it on carnal grounds it would be difficult to say. At any rate, the bulk of Mormons, from one cause or another, find themselves committed to a policy of seclusion or separatism which is repugnant to the bulk of Christians, and obviously alien to the sentiment of the United States. Either they are polygamists, or supporters of the despotic inquisitorial spiritual government of Mormonism, or they are both. Thus, though they may, and do, quarrel bitterly among themselves, any severe handling of them by Americans would produce a large party ready to resist to the death if they would preserve their institutions at all. They are fanatics by nature and choice, and would fight with the desperation of fanatics. I believe that large numbers will fall away from Mormonism, but that a body will be left sufficiently formidable to cause serious embarrassment to the authorities of the Republic. Surely the best way to correct their influence and isolated self-esteem—and, what is of great importance, to provide an escape for those who repent of Mormonism—is not to assail it by force, but to introduce and support Christian, or, as Mormons would call them, Gentile, churches in the territory. One such has been already started, amid great opposition, in the Salt Lake City. Two years and a-half ago the Protestant Episcopal Church of America sent a mission to the town. A school was opened, and 16 scholars presented themselves. Their numbers soon grew to 60. Then the Mormon authorities denounced the mission, and the school received a severe check. Presently, however, the people got over the alarm, and, in 1869, there were 130 children in the school, and the teachers could admit many more if they had room for them. Divers of the scholars were children of professing Mormons.

The sanitary condition of the city is questionable. I repeatedly asked what diseases were prevalent, and was told they were diphtheria, scarlet fever, ague, diarrhœa, and dysentery. The fact is that the lovely limpid streams that "flash through the city" are open sewers, and propagate disease among the inhabitants. I asked a man whom I knew as a resident in one of the most crowded spots in Westminster how he kept his health in Salt Lake City. " Sir," he said, " I never had a day's illness in

London, but here I have had four or five spells." "What do you drink?" I asked. "Why, the water that flows by my door." No wonder he was ill! Another said, "The grown-up people live, but lots of children die." Poor little things! I was given to understand that in many cases their parents sent for the elders of the Church to anoint them with oil, but that in their own sicknesses they took physic. I went to the chief druggist to ask, and he said he made up a great deal of medicine specially for diarrhœa; and, according to the "Salt Lake Directory," there are eight medical men residing in the city. But the babies had, I suppose, a small voice in the matter.

Another nuisance in the place, besides mischief-making surface water, arises from the flies. I never saw so many flies in my life. They crawled over our faces at breakfast by hundreds; they spotted the cloth, drowned themselves in the milk, buzzed among the dishes; and it was not until night, when they retired in black lumps to sleep upon the ceiling, that we were freed from the extreme annoyance they occasioned. These flies have their own way through the summer and autumn, and the residents seem to have made up their minds to endure their tickling inquisitiveness without complaint.

However, in spite of its drawbacks, we were deeply interested in our visit to the Mormons, especially as the present time seems to show a crisis in their history. They had just " called " about two hundred fresh missionaries, all but three of whom were to be sent out to preach in the United States. This is wise on their part, for though they make but comparatively few converts among the Yankees, it serves their purpose well to show their best side among a people who profess a strong desire for religious freedom and are yet suspected of a wish to lay heavy hands upon them before long, and " put down " polygamy, now that slavery has been swept away. But, as I have said, Brigham does not depend upon the persuasive powers of his missionaries alone. He has, Mormons say, thousands of rifles at his service in a few days if need should arise; and they will be in the hands of hardy men, who are committed, if once they begin, to fight to the last.

CHAPTER X.

THE SALT LAKE CITY.

I HAVE been asked to furnish another account of my visit to the Salt Lake City, and I furnish it at the risk of some repetition; but as I mention several matters not contained in that which precedes this, I may as well let it stand. I have said that the city lies about forty miles off the great Atlantic and Pacific Railway, but by this time is connected with it by a branch line. The railway runs by the side of the lake, which stretches far away on the left hand as you travel westward. It is one hundred miles long, by about thirty broad. Not a sail or boat was to be seen as I passed it on my way to California. The waves, however, twinkled merrily, and many gulls were flying about, while herds of cattle grazed in the saltings between the rail and the edge of the lake. Mormon farms were scattered over the plain on our right, beyond which there rose some few miles off a fine mountain range. Other mountains, patched with snow, showed themselves in the distance across the water.

The two companies whose lines together make what we call the Atlantic and Pacific Railway, meet at Promontory—this station being so named because it is on a point which juts out into the Salt Lake. I stopped to visit the City of the Saints on my way back, getting down at a little station called Uintah. The Salt Lake stage, with four greys, was waiting to take us on at once. We got seats outside, and started under a brilliant sun at twenty minutes to twelve. The lake lay on the right of our course; a range of mountains, whose lower wooded slopes were in a blaze with the bright tints of an American autumn, rose on our left. The road was the worst I ever saw. Every now and then I wondered how we could get over the watercourses, some dry, some wet, which made downright ditches athwart our track. Some we took with a rush that involved a fearful bump, for which we prepared by holding on hard; others we crossed slowly, letting the front wheels in, and then dragging them out with much straining and lashing, the hind ones following as well as they could, but at the best with a jerk which nearly "chucked" us who sat in front up into the air. I was never more jolted in my life, but I never took a drive the end of which I looked forward to with more interest, independently of its relief from rough riding. Presently we drew away from the lake, and kept closer under the hills on our left. After changing horses twice, and meeting many tilted carts with Mormons returning from their autumn gathering at the Salt Lake City, we turned a corner and saw it before us on a slope of the mountains, a grand range of which showed themselves beyond. The valley of Utah, traversed by the Jordan, and backed by another range about twenty miles off, lay on the right. As almost every house in the city has a garden and orchard, it covers a considerable space, and in the distance looks like a low wood, studded with roofs and gables. In the midst stands the Tabernacle, white and oval, like a Brobdingnag dish-cover. Last time I compared it to an egg; but whatever it may resemble, it is unlike any other building I ever saw. It has no tower, spire, or ornament of any kind within or without, but is simply a whited dish-cover, holding about 5,000 people on the floor, in benches which look towards the pulpit or platform where Brigham Young and the twelve "Apostles" sit, a large organ being behind them.

The streets of the city are very wide, unpaved and unlit. They run at right angles to each other, and on three sides die off into straight roads traversing the flat valley. The stage stopped at the post-office, and then put us down at the Townsend House, kept by a Mormon and his three wives. He has been a missionary in England, and I believe his wives are English. He was generally to be found sitting in an arm-chair in the verandah before his house, and was very polite; while one of his dames, rather a stout and stately lady in a black silk dress, looked after the maids who waited upon the guests. Mr. Townsend is a placid old gentleman, who talked freely about Mormonism to me, and took criticisms with a quiet smile. He is a man of substance. I was conversing with him one day about the schism caused by Alexander and David Smith, the sons of the founder of the "faith," when he admitted it all with the philosophic remark, "You will never find a community, sir, without divisions. We are like others in that respect." This, however, involves a serious concession; since Mormons pique themselves on unity and exclusiveness.

Many of the houses in the city, which contains about 20,000 inhabitants, are white, though some are built of "adobe," or brown sun-dried brick, there abbreviated, and pronounced "dubby." Some are large, and have their grounds fenced with high stone walls.

Streams of water run in the gutters of every street. I mentioned before that this must have an injurious sanitary effect on those who drink of them, since the seeds of disease are specially likely to be conveyed by water. I was told again and again that dysentery, diarrhœa, and fever prevailed in the place. There had been a great mortality among infants, and many residents complained of bad health. The air of the

TOWNSEND HOUSE HOTEL, SALT LAKE CITY (FROM A PHOTOGRAPH).

place is very clear, and the sunset is generally magnificent; but a sudden trying chill comes on immediately after it, however hot the day has been, and I was not surprised at being told that ague was troublesome there. The downpour of heat on the flat valley seemed to bring out a malarious haze in the evening.

We spent a good deal of our time in conversation with "promiscuous" Mormons in the stores and streets. They held much variety of opinion about polygamy, and the prospective relations of the community to the United States. Some declared that if polygamy were put down, Mormonism would perish too, and spoke very confidently about fighting the Government. I particularly remember the positiveness of one little man with a face like a weasel's. I said, " Surely you don't think you could stand against the force of the whole country?" "Sir," he replied, " the Lord will deliver us." "How?" I asked. He twinkled at me and said, "I believe that He would raise up a war between England and America, if the Government were to try and put us down by force." I suggested that I did not think England would feel gratified at such an arrangement, but he stuck fast to his notion.

Some shirked the question of polygamy by asserting that they would never think of taking more than one wife. Others admitted that though they approved of the practice, they had not adopted it in their own cases, and tried to turn off with a laugh the suggestion that they would not dare to risk the anger of the single wives they had.

I feel confident that the women, as a body, do not approve of polygamy. Of course it would be very difficult to get this admission, and indeed a stranger could not on a bare introduction ask a Mormon lady in a drawing-room whether she liked the fractional possession of a husband; but yet I heard something about it from sources which I could not doubt; and casual witness was occasionally borne to the deep aversion of the wives to this custom.

Let me give one instance of what I refer to. A Mormon of whom I had asked some questions about their prison, broke out saying that I must not suppose that Mormons ever committed crimes. "Indeed!" said I. "No, sir," he rejoined; "and I'll give you a case to show how falsely we are estimated. A man I knew was accused of embezzling his master's goods, and when the charge was gone into they found out that his wife had contrived it because he was going to marry another. It was only her spite."

I was struck how on several occasions Mormons proved too much. One day I was talking to two men, hot fanatics, about drunkenness. I asked how they punished it. "Well," one said, "we hardly ever have drunkards; but when we have we impose a fine, and in default of payment set them to work on the roads with a ball and chain." " I have not seen anything of that," I replied. "Not seen that !" he. cried; "why, there are lots. Ain't there, Jack?" he asked, appealing to his companion. I am bound to say that I did not see any drunkenness in the streets, though there are drinking-bars in the city. But no more did I even in several places where it might have been expected. However they may injure themselves by "cocktails" and "cobblers," "rum bitters" and whisky drams between meals, I must allow that throughout America I saw no gross display of intemperance in the streets. I was very much struck with the absence of this everywhere; and though I believe that Mormons are much more free from this vice than some other Western settlers, they are not unique among Americans in abstaining from public exhibitions of it.

I am inclined to believe, moreover, that fanaticism is sometimes a sort of alternative to material intoxication. People who are filled with a pressing sense of strong and peculiar religious convictions are less subject to that craving and depression which affects those who lead a dull, spiritless life. There is no doubt of the sincerity with which the bulk of Mormons hold their strange creed. It is a very strange one indeed, but it has stimulated many of them not only to break away from their old life, but in some instances to make their journey to Utah a sort of religious pilgrimage. Thus they are delivered more or less from a yearning for physical stimulants.

It might be suggested that in the practice of polygamy they find another species of indulgence; and in some instances no doubt this is true, especially since plural marriage is not part of their original code of life, and many have adopted it with readiness on the ground of a later revelation. I can find no directions for it in the "Book of Mormon" which I purchased at the Salt Lake City, while it is distinctly forbidden in the "Book of Doctrine and Covenants" in circulation in the territory of Utah now. The words—I quote from the copy I bought there—are in section cix., on "Marriage," and run thus—"Inasmuch as this Church of Christ has been reproached with the crime of fornication, and polygamy; we declare that we believe that one man should have one wife, and one woman but one husband, except in case of death, when either is at liberty to marry again." This is "selected from the Revelations of God, by Joseph Smith, President," and is in the stereotyped edition, published in 1854.

Now, when Brigham Young announced that he had in his possession a revelation superseding this and recommending polygamy, which revelation he said he had kept back because the Church was not ripe to receive it, we must assume a monstrous readiness to adopt a practice which is said to prevail among about sixty thousand of the Mormon community at the present day. These polygamists have committed themselves in the face of the prohibition which still stands in the "Book of Doctrine and Covenants" current among them.

I am afraid that unbridled passions have had a good deal to do with what is now defended among many as a Divine duty, and that though Mormons are not drunkards, some have seriously damaged their character for temperance by their unblushing adoption of a practice that is more than bigamous.

I do not want to paint any one blacker than he is, but it is notorious that some Mormons, pure and simple, represented mainly by the sons of the original prophet, two of whom, David and Alexander Smith, were at the Salt Lake City, protest against polygamy. I mentioned in a previous chapter that I heard Alexander Smith, at a crowded meeting of Mormons, denounce Brigham Young's teaching in this matter as "false, foul, and corrupt."

Mormons are now divided into "Josephites" and "Brighamites," the former of whom denounce the latter unsparingly. Here is native internal testimony to the corrupt morality of the sect. No language can express a sense of the "abomination" of polygamy more strongly than that which is now being used by the original Mormons, who are the opponents of Brigham Young in the very heart of his empire.

I say empire, because he undoubtedly exercises imperial power over a very large section of the Mormons, and is backed by all those who have been induced by his example and precepts to take more wives than one. If polygamy were abolished, they would be in a social strait. Thus they are prepared to fight for—I can hardly call it their liberty—but their license. I was told that they had some 18,000 men well armed and organised. They were preparing to assemble when I was in Utah. This was intended as a hint of what would happen if the United States were to attempt to put down polygamy by force. I have no doubt that forcible suppression of this practice is contemplated by many Americans. Divers said to me, "Well, sir, we shall fix this matter up before long." But it will be, if tried, a serious business. I have since learned that measures have been taken to suppress the Mormon militia. Still they have pugnacity among them. Many, as I have remarked, believe now that if polygamy were suppressed, Mormonism would perish. Thus they have social and religious motives to support them. Moreover the ecclesiastical system pursued by Brigham Young is so minutely imperious that he has more than the polygamists under his thumb. Organised subdivision of the " Church," under apostles, bishops, and teachers, enables him to check at once any material opposition or conspiracy. No one can move freely. The sons of Joseph Smith are listened to; but it is hard to begin any revolution. Families and individuals are watched and reported upon. If disobedient they are excommunicated, and that means that they are denied work and help.

It is difficult to see how the compact body of polygamists, and that society of non-polygamists who are subjected with them to the same tyrannical supervision, can be broken up. I believe that there are elements of dissolution in the growth of the schism fostered by the sons of Joseph Smith. This is likely to encourage the belief that there are two sides to Mormonism. Then comes in the influence of other teaching, shown already by the success which has attended the efforts of the Episcopal clergy in the heart of Utah. But, if hard pressed, divided Mormons may shake hands again.

Extract from a Letter, dated Nov. 4, 1870, to the Author of " San Francisco and Back."

THE writer, the Rev. G. W. Foote, the Rector of the Church Mission at the Salt Lake City, after speaking of the need he has for help to complete the building of his church, with schools, clergy-house, &c., says:—

" The Mormon problem is being gradually solved

by the constant defections of the people. . . . The United States courts have recently declared all Mor-, mon courts illegal, and their actions null and void. Our new governor . . . has forbidden the Mormon militia to meet, and has taken the power into his own hands, reducing Brigham Young to a mere ecclesiastical head of Mormonism. We have also obtained good judges and a 'Gentile' jury. These judges refuse to naturalise polygamists or those who believe in polygamy, and our juries have indicted some prominent Mormons (a bishop among them) for murders committed years ago.

"The mines (silver) all about our city are attracting much attention, and we expect that thousands of people will rush in here next spring. Already the territory is fast filling up with 'Gentile' miners, and thousands of dollars are being taken from the mines. The Mormon railway is completed from Ogden to this city, and hundreds of travellers pass through here weekly.

"Our congregations have increased in numbers, and our school has been enlarged also ; we now have six teachers and 230 pupils."

I must say a word on the natural resources of the place. Much has been made of the transformation by the Saints of a barren wilderness into a blooming field. This is nonsense. Of course land will not

grow useful crops before it is sown. But little more
is needed in the valley of Utah than to till and plant
soil aided by a magnificent sun and supplies of water
from all sides. I have open before me now the "Salt
Lake Directory," given to me there by a Mormon,
and which contains their own account of their progress
in that region. The "Chronological Events of Utah"
has this as its first statement: "1847· July 24.
Pioneers, numbering 143 men, enter Salt Lake
Valley, having left the Missouri River April 14th.
The day of their arrival they commenced ploughing
and planting potatoes. A thunder-shower wet the
ground slightly in the afternoon." A few lines below
this we read: "July 31. Great Salt Lake City laid
out in square blocks of ten acres each." A few lines
lower still: "August 26. The colonists had laid off
a fort, built twenty-seven log houses, ploughed and
planted eighty-four acres with corn, potatoes, beans,
buck-wheat, turnips, &c., and had manufactured 125
bushels of salt." The salt they got from the lake
pools. The bringing eighty-four acres under cultivation a month after their arrival proves that they found
soil ready for farming. Such is the case on their
own showing. Utah is a grand field for agriculture.
The triumph of saintly labour over stubborn Nature is
a mere myth. Everything was as ready for them as
it could be. While I was there I saw Mormon
farmers breaking up fresh soil. They simply ploughed

it. I should add that Nature herself provides much grass for pasturage.

I drove and walked about the neighbourhood of the city, which is beautifully situated. The territory produces almost everything—fruit, corn, roots, sugar-cane, cotton, silk, coal, ores. It is not a reclaimed wilderness, but was in one sense an unclaimed paradise when the Mormons entered it.

Its seclusion is now gone. But the railroad had to creep more than a thousand miles from the banks of the Missouri, across plains in which the buffalo and Red Indian still wander, over the Rocky Mountains, and through the barren, stony land which lies beyond them, before the snort of the engine was heard in the smiling valley of Utah. My companion and myself were among the last to traverse the vile road between the main line and the Salt Lake City. Now a branch is opened, and you may go by rail into the heart of the town. I am much mistaken if some summer tourists will not change their trip among the familiar scenes of Europe for a visit to this place, and see for themselves the homes of the " Latter-day Saints : " of them we have heard much and shall hear more.

CHAPTER XI.

RETURN JOURNEY.

I TURNED off to St. Louis on the Missouri from the terminus of the Pacific Union line at Omaha. On my way back from the Salt Lake City I was even more impressed with the solitary ambition of the line which has pushed its way across the continent than I was in my outward journey, for I happened to travel in the end car of the train, and could thus see the straight thin track, looking at last no bigger than a piece of string stretched across, say Dartmoor, or Salisbury Plain. On our return, too, we saw the prairie on fire; but it was daytime, and the effect was simply an horizon of smoke. The fire had passed close to the line; indeed, some of it was blazing only a few hundred yards off. The flames were in places about ten or twelve feet high, but, curiously enough, many of the tall, strong bents of grass were left standing in the blackened track of the conflagration.

When we got back to Omaha, I left the direct route to Chicago and turned down the Missouri by the

ATLANTIC AND PACIFIC RAILROAD, FROM TOP OF ROCKY MOUNTAINS, ABOVE SHERMAN STATION, SHOWING THE BROKEN TABLE-LAND FROM THAT POINT (FROM A PHOTOGRAPH).

Hannibal and St. Joseph Railway, which runs along what is called the Missouri Bottom. A word about this line. It is abominable. Accidents occur about once a-week. I happened to say to a fellow-passenger, "We shall get to St. Joseph, I suppose, about such and such an hour." "Well, yes," he replied, "if they don't run off the track." My first indication of this habit of the train here occurred when I took my ticket for a sleeping-berth. The clerk gave me one for a Pullman car. On going on the platform I saw no Pullman, but one of another sort. "How's this?" I asked of the conductor; "I've got a ticket for a Pullman." "Well, sir," said he, "if you have got the ticket you should have the car." He didn't tell me that their one Pullman had just been left standing on its head at the bottom of an embankment. However, we started, and had not gone far before our train ran off the line too. One poor fellow had both his thighs broken, and we were detained about three hours, and had to leave our engine. I believe it was in a ditch, but being fast asleep all through the accident, I did not learn about it till some hours afterwards. It is curious how one can sleep through such a jar as we had. Soon after I woke we just missed an ugly collision. I was on the platform at the end of the car, and seeing the train coming, jumped off, naturally; but the danger was averted. As many as could, though, jumped out of the train, there being no risk in so doing, as our part was hardly moving.

The route by the Missouri is very dismal in places, The river is probably one of the ugliest in the world— a muddy, shallow, wide stream, with great expanse of mud banks bristling with the trunks and arms of dead trees. Ague reigns supreme here. Again and again we passed by the site of the Eden in "Martin Chuzzlewit." There were great breadths of flat, wet shore, indented by lagoons of deadly-looking water, in which stood a tangled growth of trees surrounded by rotting fallen branches and slimy weeds, the site of which desolation had never been touched since the continent of America rose out of the primeval seas.

But where the waters had subsided and left arable soil the crops were monstrous. I do not know whether my readers will believe me, but yet it is a fact that some of the stalks of the Indian corn were 15 feet high. As I sat in the train while it passed along an embankment, the tops of the stems growing in the field below rose in several instances above my head. A friend, an accurate and trustworthy man, told me he had measured stalks of corn which were 17 feet long. Indeed, the energy and resource of some of these virgin soils are almost incredible.

Our progress was slow through the Missouri Bottom, as the line runs in part through coarse pastures, and there being no fence, the cattle were constantly getting on the line. These had to be "tooted" at emphatically by our trumpet-whistle, and sometimes the train was pulled up, since the cows simply set off waddling down the line before us, as if, naturally enough, they thought they could go at least as fast as anything on the Hannibal and St. Joseph Railway.

At last, late in the second day, we reached St. Charles, about 20 miles from St. Louis, where the Missouri had to be crossed by the train. There was no bridge, but a huge dirty ferry-boat, with all its machinery above deck. This, churning up the yellow water, took over three cars at a time, each about 50 feet long. The Missouri flows into the Mississippi about four or five miles below this. It was quite dark before we got off on the other side of the river, and all we saw of St. Louis on entering was a twinkle of lights.

This is a busy city, with main avenues running parallel to the Mississippi, and intersected by streets at right angles to it. It is smokier than any part of London, and therefore dirty. It is a steady rival to Chicago, and there is much interchange of jealous comparisons between the two cities, but Chicago is by far the most thriving place. St. Louis is, in fact, quite ancient, being some 100 years old. The day after my arrival I went down at once to look at the famous river. A heavy cloud of smoke and fog hung

MISSISSIPPI STEAMBOAT (FROM A PHOTOGRAPH).

over it, and on the St. Louis side lay a fringe of great
white high-pressure steamboats, with tiers of decks
and two tall funnels each. I had intended to descend
the river from this place to Cairo, but desisted, not
fancying the steamboats. And thus I was possibly
saved from being one of the passengers on board one
which I looked at as it lay ready to sail. It was
burned on that very trip, and some 150 passengers
lost their lives.

I spent the Sunday in St. Louis. It is called by
some the City of Churches. The Episcopal Church
here, though, is weak. I asked the clerk in the
office of the Planters' House where I stopped, who
were the great preachers in the town. He replied
that they were all burning and shining lights; so I
went to one large Episcopal church, where it struck
me, however, that there was not much warmth.
After visiting the Sunday-school, I took my place in
a very fashionable congregation; the church, like
almost all I have seen in America, being made as
comfortable as stoves, carpets, and cushions could
make it. The choir, as usual, sat in the organ-loft,
and consisted of ladies and gentlemen, who were but
little accompanied by the congregation. The sermon
was quiet and practical, but the whole tone of the
service was coldly respectable. The street in which
the church stood seemed to be almost dedicated to
religion, and they told me its title was to be changed

from "Locust," a favourite street name in the States, to "Church" Street. The large number of places of worship in all American cities is very striking. The newness of them is as remarkable as their abundance. Many look as if they had been finished last week. Though young, they are built to last, being in most cases in the cities constructed of brick or stone. Country churches are generally built of wood, and as ugly as they can be built. In this respect they are like almost all the houses in the country, which are wooden and painted white, seeming, as one remarks, to have no root in the ground.

I have said that the service in the Episcopal Church I worshipped in at St. Louis was coldly respectable. By this, however, I do not mean that it seemed worse than that in those of other denominations. In one Western city I looked into—I think it was—eight churches and chapels on the Sunday. Everywhere appeared the same extreme comfort in the matter of seats and carpets, but with the exception of one, a Baptist chapel, where the singing was fairly congregational, all had the same chilly religious atmosphere. Indeed, there is a silence and sadness about most American assemblages, so far as I have seen them. And this includes the gatherings for meals in hotels. A hundred Americans dining in public do so generally with an air more suited to an examination in mathematics than to a meal which ought to be cheery. I have repeatedly been struck, by contrast, with the character which we have as natives of "merry" England. Almost all Americans take iced water or weak tea at dinner, and no wine or beer. But at odd times they drink oceans of "bitters" and "syrups." No wonder they are melancholy!

CHAPTER XII.

PAUPERISM.—NEGRO LABOUR.

AFTER a day or two in St. Louis, I took my ticket for Philadelphia, a singularly rectangular city, by Cincinnati and Pittsburg, along what is called the Pan Handle route—so named because it crosses a narrow neck of Virginia, like, on the map, the handle of a frying-pan. The road is good. We came at an excellent pace, and were only about two hours after our time.

The country is flat or slightly undulating most of the way, till you begin to draw towards the Alleghanies, some kindred ranges of which run through the eastern, central, and southern parts of Pennsylvania. But I have a word more about St. Louis before I get to Cincinati on my way into this State. I occupied myself before I started from St. Louis with inquiries about the price of provisions, going into the baker's shops, stopping the milkman on his rounds, &c. The milk was eight cents a quart : a cent is about a halfpenny. I was surprised at the price of bread—ten cents for a loaf a little less than 2 lb. weight. I wandered into the poorest part of the town, and felt that any emigrating

from the slums of our cities might easily find themselves at home in the close alleys and rooms of this
place. The smells, moreover, of the poor parts of
every American city I have been in are much the
same as in London; in divers cases worse. Indeed,
I think that the sanitary condition of some of the
poor parts of London, as far as my observations have
guided me, is ahead of those in the New World. I
am speaking of such as exhibit signs of science and
care. The much-praised and beautifully placed Salt
Lake City is miserably arranged, as far as health
goes. The streams which flow through the streets
are simply sewers. They run fast and twinkle in the
sun, but for all that they carry the seeds of disease
about the place. But the City of the Saints is no
fair test of American progress. It has not, *e.g.*, even
a lamp in the streets. I am speaking of such towns
as St. Louis, Cincinnati, and Philadelphia. I have
prowled about these, and come on smells which
brought the Seven Dials forcibly to mind. With all
this, I am bound to say that I have not found
anywhere the sodden, tattered element of population
which disgraces London. Nor, with the exception of
two beggars in Philadelphia who stopped me in the
street, have I as yet been asked by any one for alms.
I ought to mention, though, that blind men sometimes board the trains, and little children come into
the reading-rooms of the hotels for what they can

get. But they do not pester you. They simply come in with a suppliant face and walk round, holding out their hands. The philanthropy of Philadelphia and New York is, however, producing its harvest of paupers, and they say that during the winter the begging in these places, specially the latter, has already grown to be very considerable. Once hereabouts, on being introduced to an active philanthropist, he said to me, "We have not the destitution of London here, sir:" as if, like the manager of a performance, he were apologising for some imperfection. I ventured to console him by saying that I thought he and his friends were manufacturing it fast. He didn't seem to see it, and looked surprised at my rejoinder. But though, with the enthusiasm of nascent impulsive philanthropy, he could not deny that beggary was growing, he looked as if he would have liked to question my comment—and I have had considerable experience in begging and the careless " charity" which promotes it—but he made no reply. I hope he thought the more. The beggars, though, have not shown themselves, as in London, wherever I have been in America, nor are there any crossing-sweepers. The slow, splashed, dilapidated men who sweep the streets early in the morning are, I suppose, cosmopolitan. I have, in America, come on gangs of them precisely similar to our own in London; and they get much about the same wages as with us. I think I have already mentioned that I did not see or hear an itinerant organ grinder. There were a few street organs, but they were ground mostly by maimed soldiers, who were fixed to one corner of a street and sat, with their instruments, on the ground. I once saw two on the opposite corners of the same thorough-fare. They had placards saying in what battle they were wounded, and each played different tunes all day, at the same time, at either end of the same crossing.

To return. Knowing that the country was quite level between St. Louis and Cincinnati, I crossed it by night in a sleeping-car, and woke to find myself on a dead flat, set with patches of small timber, the everlasting Indian corn, and pumpkins. The road ran as straight as an arrow, and the same white wooden houses and villages as ever were scattered about the country. There was not a hill, mound, or eminence of any sort in sight; and all the farming, as usual, was coarse and untidy.

There were, however, many signs that we had left the rough West for a State which had long been settled. The character of the crowd of wayfarers and men about the stations was changed. There were no unkempt "boys" with wide hat, flannel shirt, trousers stuck into boots, and strong leather belt, suggestive of the six-shooter and knife which hung behind. People, however, are emigrating from Ohio into the wondrous West.   The New England farmers, on the contrary, are in many cases selling all that they have and buying land in the South, where it might be had, of the best, while I was there, for eight or ten dollars an acre, and negro labour could be obtained for some ten dollars a month and coarse board—meal and bacon; whereas in the West the labourer, in the summer, often gets thirty dollars a month, and better board than is given to the negro.   Moreover the New Englander, by going south, has not to put up with the loss of civilisation like the man who leaves an old settled district to make a fresh home in the new districts of Nebraska, Kansas, and the like.

CHAPTER XIII.

CINCINNATI AND PHILADELPHIA.

I got to Cincinnati at a little after nine in the morning, and, thanks to the covenient usage in the matter of railway tickets, "lay over" there for a day. The American plan, by which you can buy a ticket at your hotel if you like, or at least in some office hard by, is much better than ours. For instance, at San Francisco I bought my ticket for New York, paying no more for coming round by St. Louis. I used it first to Stockton. Then I had it in my pocket-book during a ten days' excursion into the Sierra Nevada on horseback. On striking the line again, I was not obliged to have it stamped or re-dated, but at every station it came out as good as new; and I might have stopped for three months, and still travelled on without troubling myself more than to show it, when called upon, to the conductor of the train. At the risk of more repetition, too, I must record the perpetually repeated favourable impression caused by the luggage system. I had a trunk, bought in San Francisco, which I choked with a lot of things from

Chinese shops, the Yo Semite Valley—cones, bark, &c., a heavy parcel, containing buffalo robes, &c., and a bag. My trunk, &c., I sent on 2,000 miles. My bag I kept with me. Whenever I wanted to stop a day or two at a place, I had only to speak to an authorised "express man" on board the train. I handed him the brass check which had a corresponding one on the bag, and when I had secured my room at the hotel, my bag walked in at once without more ado. Moreover, while travelling, I several times wanted something out of my big bag. I had only to walk along inside the train to the baggage-van, knock at the door, and, showing my check, ask leave to open my luggage and take out - what I needed. Every facility is thus given to travellers in the matter of tickets and baggage, and the people who look after your interests are always civil. When I got near New York I had only to give my checks to the polite "express man," and I then simply handed him my railway-rug and hand-bag in the train, some half-hour before my arrival. I then only took a street car, six cents, to my hotel, and my things were laid out in my room for me as soon as possible. Any one, however, who tried, as some do at first, to look after his luggage in the English fashion, would be sorely perplexed. Generally the stations seem to be without porters, and you don't know whom to ask any question of. You must settle all your luggage

business before you get out of the train. If you
think to keep guard over your own things and see
them put into the van without checks, intending to
see them taken out, you will be disappointed. The
luggage-master in the train will simply put them out
at the next station on the platform, and leave them
there. This is a land of minute regulations. Any
assertion of British independence in the matter of
self-protection is quietly ignored. I saw all the
luggage of one man turned out by the wayside at a
station in the West, because he had neglected to
observe the usual routine. A departure from this
will surely get the traveller into trouble.

Cincinnati is a religious city, though the reading of
the Bible was some time ago, by an unholy combina-
tion of Jews, Freethinkers, and Roman Catholics,
excluded from the common schools.* I had two sets
of tracts and cards put into my hands before I got
outside the railway station.

I turned my steps at once to the Ohio, which is
here crossed by a suspension bridge of 1,200 feet
span, at a great height above the river. The water
was rather low, and the business of smoothing and
paving the wide sloping banks was going busily on.
There was, as usual in these river-side American
cities, a border of white, large, high-backed steamers,

---

* This act of exclusion has, I understand, since then been
rescinded.

with double funnel, and the machinery naked above deck; the pilot's steering-box, like a smart little summer-house in a tea-garden, being raised up on high, and "dominating" the whole concern in the midst. I was going to say that Cincinnati was the smokiest town I ever saw, but Pittsburgh beats it in floating dirt. It calls itself the " Queen City of the West," but is often named "Porcopolis," being a great centre of hog slaughtering. Of course, here I expected to find pork cheap, but was astonished to find that it sells at eighteen cents per pound. I am at a loss to account for the very high retail price of provisions wherever I go. At Chicago mutton was decidedly cheap by the carcase, but small quantities of meat are everywhere dear. At New York they pay from thirty-five to forty cents per pound for beef-steaks, not so good as English. At Cincinnati I found prime cuts of beef and mutton were fifteen cents a pound, potatoes sixty cents a bushel, brown sugar seventeen or eighteen cents a pound, bread five cents, coffee thirty to thirty-five, tea a dollar and a half, and "table" butter forty-five cents. I got these prices by going into shops, like a customer, and asking the prices. Wages are higher than with us. A bricklayer gets six dollars a day, but is generally out of work half the year. Carpenters have four dollars a day; ordinary labourers about two dollars. Rents are very high. I asked a man who served me in a shop what he paid. He said three rooms on the second floor cost him fifteen dollars a month, and that a cottage with three rooms and a kitchen was twenty dollars a month. A working man paid twelve dollars a month for two rooms, or about ten shillings a week, allowing for the depreciation of the currency. All the prices I have given are in currency, but they seem to show that in *cities* it is doubtful if artisans gain by emigration from England to America. I should add that clothing is about three times as dear there as with us. Here, though, I found no squalid class. All seem to have work, and the city was full of business. A barber, however, who brushed my hair, talked of improving his condition by going to England. I have been very much struck again and again by the respectful way in which people speak of the old country.

I have talked in the train, in steamboats, in shops, hotels, and at street corners, with men of all sorts— with, indeed, everyone who would enter into conversation with me: in America you generally have to break the ice yourself, since very few people speak to their travelling neighbours, whether native or not; and almost invariably free complaint is made of the heavy, provoking taxes which are laid upon the people, the jobbery of officials, and the corruption of justice. These are the three leading phases of grumbling. Almost every one says that Judges and members of Congress can be bribed. They may be right or wrong in their persuasion, but all I can say is that I have hardly talked with an American on these matters who did not thus abuse the working of the institutions of his country. He will dwell upon its resources, its bigness, its power, its incalculable future, but he will have his fling at the Legislature.

While at Sacramento I strolled into a place of entertainment where comic dialogues were held between coloured men, and almost all the jokes, those which drew most applause, were levelled at the rulers of the land. A "curiosity" long discussed turned out to be "a Massachusetts General who did not steal spoons." Another man injured his brains by an accident and left them to be mended at a shop, but forgot to call for them because he happened to be elected as a national legislator and did not observe their absence, &c. Thus joke after joke was turned against the Legislature, or the Army, or the absurdity of asking for Alabama "clams," or a "Finnicom" invasion of Canada when the English soldiers "arrested" everything down to what was very like the vermin which accompanied the invaders.

On the subject of Fenians I was much interested. I pulled out the Fenian stop on every possible occasion, and I never met with an American who did not speak of Fenians with the strongest contempt. They dislike them much, but find their vote convenient on the eve of elections. Of course, divers Irishmen had a different opinion of Fenianism.

When practicable, I also drew the conversation to the subject of repudiation, and altogether I met with only two who desired it. I need hardly say that an American has generally an opinion, and is never slow to admit it when asked; but over and over again I have heard some such sentiments as this— "Repudiate, sir! Nonsense; where would the credit of the country be?" There is, we know, a party which advocates repudiation, but I must say what I have heard.

I mention this now because on the journey from St. Louis I happened to have an extra amount of conversation with my fellow travellers on political affairs.

Another thing that struck me on this journey was the number of rivers which water the country in these parts. Besides the Susquehanna, the Juniata, the Schuylkill, the Delaware, the Ohio, &c., we saw or crossed many of which my fellow passengers could not tell me the names.

The Alleghanies form a very picturesque range of mountains, but are tame. They are mostly wooded, and the autumn tints of the leaves were exceedingly beautiful, yet they present no striking forms on the sky-line, and are very much like themselves. Many portions of our route, though, especially where the railroad followed the course of rivers, were more than pretty. I was much amused by a fellow-traveller who, as we came on a remarkably fine and distant valley view, with cliffs of rock, &c., said to me, " There, sir; there is nothing to beat that in Switzerland." I said I missed the mountains and the snow and the ice and the lakes, and asked him to which part of Switzerland he referred. " Well, sir," he replied; " I have been there." " So have I," I rejoined, and ran through the names of some dozen or so of Swiss districts with which I am familiar. He got up and walked off to the other end of the car in disgust, which, if not un-speakable, was, at least on this occasion, unspoken.

I did not come across much bragging, but when I did find some, it was full-grown.

Philadelphia, where I stayed, is a distressingly correct and beautiful city. The houses are mostly of red brick, and brilliant with advertisements. The vistas down the main streets are fine, the shops are excellent, and the people all seem respectable. Numerous street-cars run in every thoroughfare, and the foot pavements are in places of red brick, like the houses. There are many trees in the city, their green contrasting beautifully with the prevailing red of the houses.

I will not pause to tell you of divers stock sights which I went to see, comprising among other things the table on which the Declaration of Independence was signed, &c., for these are the standing dishes of Philadelphia; but I must make mention of my visit to the Sunday-School Jubilee of the Methodist Episcopal Church, which was held during my stay here in the Academy of music—in other words a large theatre.

The "Methodist Episcopal Church" is the most numerous Protestant community in the United States, numbering about five times as many as the "Protestant Episcopal." Bishop Simpson is, I believe, its senior— at least its chief pastor. He was to be present at this Jubilee : and as President Grant is also a member of this Church, and was then a visitor in the city, his presence was also secured at the Jubilee, which thus became of special importance and interest. I took my place in the theatre, one among 4,000 or 5,000 who filled every corner and gallery of the building. A portion of the Sunday-School scholars from a number of chapels were seated on the stage. They comprised 1,100 girls, many of them grown young women, in white dresses, and the crowd of them reached as far back as the space behind the footlights could be cleared out to accommodate them. They entirely covered the floor of the stage, and as they mostly fanned themselves as they sat ready for the proceedings to begin, the sight, from the middle of the lower gallery, where I sat, was very striking. One of the stage boxes was reserved for the President,

PHILADELPHIA (FROM A PHOTOGRAPH).

and the hum of conversation broke into clapping of
hands and cheers when he appeared and took his
seat, accompanied by Mrs. Grant and a party of
friends.

Bishop Simpson then stood facing the audience in
front of the conductor's seat and offered a short
sensible prayer, and the proceedings, which consisted
of songs and recitations by the scholars, some
religious, some comic, commenced. The singing was
not good; it lacked the fulness and the light and
shade of similar school choruses in England. Part
of it, moreover, was simply painful, at least to myself.
On more than one occasion two scholars were brought
forward to sing a duet. They were horribly frightened,
poor girls, and made no more noise than two mice in
a barn. Of course, their untrained voices could not
fill the building. They were heard and seen, that
was all; and some of the audience cheered good-
humouredly. But the sense of failure was somewhat
effaced by about thirty infant scholars, who sang a
song called the " Jolly little Clacker." These little
trots had no sense of shyness, and did their very best,
standing in a row behind the foot-lights, and clapping
their hands in accompaniment to the refrain—which
was—

> Click, click, click, clack, clack, clack,
> Jolly little clacker, with your clack, clack, clack.

Then they all bobbed a curtsey, and were trooped out

by a teacher. The clacker is, I believe, an American bird.

But the President was there, and the chance of dragging him into the performance was too great to be lost. He is very shy and reserved, but he is the President, and a member of the " Methodist Episcopal Church," so he had to gratify his friends.

One of the songs, far on in the programme, was " See the conquering hero," &c. This they took out of its turn, and compelled the President to assist in rendering effective. They led him out of his box and set him behind one of the scenes about one-third of the way down the stage. There he stood looking very uncomfortable till the verse began—" See the god-like youth advancing." Then he marched out to a chair in the middle, directly in front of the footlights, and sat down with a big nosegay in his hand, looking still more out of his element. After the song, the people insisted on a speech from him. He is a very wise man, and seldom speaks in public; but they were too much for him on this occasion. He therefore got up and made a few remarks, in a tone so low that some of the audience were rude enough to shout " Speak louder!" But he did not, choosing rather to shut his mouth and sit down. Then he was asked to walk towards the back of the stage, and either see or show himself to the scholars, the young ladies in white. This he did; but the temptation was too strong for the damsels, who presently made a rush upon him **and** devoured him, falling upon him in such force that presently I could see only the top of his head—he is very short—in a whirlpool of white muslin. The scene was so ludicrous that a general cackle of laughter rose from the whole audience, and the poor President swam out as fast as he could, leaving the theatre immediately afterwards. The spectators were much pleased, a lady next me passing into a state of great excitement at the osculation, and lending me her opera-glass that I might see it better. The whole thing was a success, and an Institution for the Aged and Infirm reaped a good harvest from the receipts. I paid half-a-dollar for admission.

CHAPTER XIV.

A SHORT RUN SOUTHWARD.

I was enabled to pay a short visit to Washington and Richmond. I went by night straight to the latter place from New York, and stopped in Washington on my way back. The convenience of these sleeping-cars, &c., cannot be mentioned too often, as, say what we will, England must learn a lesson from America in the matter of material provision for the comfort of travellers; while I wish she may learn from us to provide a more careful set of officials to drive and conduct trains. The carriages, &c., are excellent, but the staff is often frightfully careless of injury to public limbs and life. And then the papers do not report accidents as they ought. Shortly after I had crossed the continent by the Atlantic and Pacific rail a terrible collision occurred upon it, for accounts of which I looked in vain into the columns of the *New York Times, Herald,* and *Tribune.* The accident was caused by gross neglect. A passenger train had run off the rails in consequence of a defective switch, which had been reported—so I heard—as out of

N

order. It was got on again after some hours, messengers with signals being sent back. But the driver of an emigrant train wholly disregarded them, and running full smash into the stationary passenger train, killed six or seven persons, and wounded many others. The voice of public opinion at least ought to have been heard loudly on such an occasion; but, as I said, I looked for it in vain. I may have missed comments which were made; I did not find them. A gentleman who was present at the disaster told us that on asking the conductor what mischief was done, he received the reply, "One passenger and six Mormons killed, and twenty wounded." The accident happened in a most dreary part of the route, where the poor people had to wait for hours before a surgeon could be got, and he was found only among the passengers of another train.

To return, I took my berth in a sleeping-car in the train which left New York at 9 P.M., and after travelling 226 miles while asleep, woke in Washington. Then I went at once on board a steamer, which runs about sixty miles down the Potomac to Acquia Creek, the water base of the long military operations against the lines of Richmond.

The Potomac has slightly elevated wooded banks, and is a broad, beautiful river, looking, I fancied, even wider than it is. Here were no mud shores bristling with dead timber as on the Mississippi and the Missouri, but headlands rich with autumn-tinted trees. We steamed rapidly down, and soon reached our landing-place, now a mere railway station on a wooden pier. A large number of charred piles holding their black heads above the water showed where the Government stores had stood. People in the boat said they had been burnt by Federals in office after the war, in order to secure a price for their contents to some contractors.

I had looked forward with much interest to the seeing of some relics of the war, and now we had to cross a country which had long been the scene of repeated battle. It is undulating, and very desolate. Farmers before the war had worked their land till it lost heart, and now it waits for Northern capital. The scattered patches of corn were most miserable in comparison with what I had seen along the Missouri bottom. I should correct an impression which may perhaps have been made by my statement that some of the corn-stalks there were fifteen feet high. I referred to maize, which is always called "corn" in America; other grain being known only as wheat, barley, and the like.

"On board" the train from Acquia Creek to Richmond I found myself for the first time during my tour among those with Southern opinions. On happening to ask a gentleman as we landed whether he had been in the war, he replied, "Yes, sir; I was a rebel, and

you will soon see the graveyards I helped to fill."
Then he chuckled, and added, "But we can't do
without the North now. They have the capital, we
have land and labour."

Signs of war soon showed themselves in breast-
works, &c., looking almost as fresh as when they were
made. We stopped some little time at Fredericksburg, on the opposite bank of the Rappahannock, a
comparatively narrow river for America. The town
is now well mended, though there are many patches;
and I saw one or two skeletons of houses still untouched. I was struck by the very great increase in
the number of negroes visible everywhere. My bitter
Southern companion said they lived by stealing. We
saw the cemetery, filled mainly after the battle of
Fredericksburg. It is kept in most scrupulous order,
each grave being marked by a white headstone with
the names, where they could be ascertained, of the
soldiers buried in them. As these white memorials
were placed in rows at equal distances and covered
several acres, the effect was unpleasantly prim, the
place looking like a large nursery ground stuck full
of labels. It sorely wanted the air of consecration
which is associated with the resting-places of the dead.
All was clean, neat, and uniform, but staring and
unmournful. It seemed at the first glance to have no
indication of individual sorrow, but it was certainly
marked by the sign of national care. Here I may

AN AMERICAN CEMETERY (FROM A PHOTOGRAPH).

say that whilst descending the Potomac the bell of
the steamer tolled as we passed Mount Vernon, the
home and tomb of Washington. The rail between
Acquia Creek and Richmond has been repaired
throughout since the war, but, as usual, has no fence.
Hence we were checked in several places by cattle
on the line, and once we ran foul of a poor beast
of a bull, which we cut down, the " cow-catcher "
on the bows of the engine flinging it off the track.
Occasionally the cattle are avenged by keeping
their own carcases on the line and throwing the
train off.

The part of Virginia we passed through had much
the same appearance all along the route. The lines
of Richmond, of yellow earth, are mostly as marked
as ever; and when I looked back from the top of the
Capitol at the country we had crossed, I saw them
stretching away right and left out of sight. The
situation of Richmond is very picturesque, the James
River above the town being thickly studded with
islands. The burnt district is mainly rebuilt, and
the whole city was alive with a fair or exhibition, in
which agricultural implements and produce held a
very prominent place. Plasterers and whitewashers,
too, were, as a negro there said, " fixing up " the
Capitol " a bit." It is of Grecian architecture, and
the most conspicuous object in the city, being set on a
hill, whence it commands a fine view of the town and

its surroundings. It has, however, both inside and out, an air of desolation and decay.

We visited the Libby Prison, on the river-bank, a square dismal edifice, with three large floors. In one sense it keeps up the sentiment of its business when it was crowded with half-famished Federal prisoners, for it is converted into a bone-crushing manufactory. There was a propriety, too, in the use now made of the old slave-market. There it stood, the same as ever; only, instead of offering "hands" for sale, it was bright with a great advertisement of "Excelsior reaping mowing-machines," and the floor was cumbered with good store of agricultural implements. I noticed also divers shops devoted to the provision of farm seeds, &c. Altogether Richmond seems to have made a great rise out of its fall, and the buildings erected on the site of the burnt district, though the walls are patchy with the blackened bricks used in their construction, indicate a prosperous commercial future. The suburbs and outer streets of the city, with their sober-looking, weather-worn red brick detached houses, reminded me more of an old English town than anything I had seen in America. The inn, too, had some air of the old country, the landlord making a point of thanking us when we left his house—a piece of politeness which you are not likely to hear from the attendants or managers of a large roaring hotel, however civil they may be.

I returned to Washington in a train filled with people who had visited the fair, but as I happened to travel in a car fitted, as some are, with cane easy chairs, instead of the usual seats, there was no crowding, each passenger having a place to himself. These chairs are very luxurious, as you can let down the back to your own angle, and have plenty of room to stretch your legs.

Washington, called the "city of magnificent distances," is a very striking sketch of a metropolis. The streets are wider than any I ever saw, and being both very long and straight, fill you with a sense of perspective. Everything is on the largest scale, but it is a skeleton, the number of houses bearing a small proportion to the site of the city. The public buildings are very fine, but almost painfully white. The streets are so arranged that many vistas are closed by one of these edifices, the Capitol being everywhere most conspicuous. It is an immense structure, but very grand in its proportions. It looks as if it had been finished the day before, and washed that morning. The appearance of its dome is familiar to our readers, but its whiteness is even more staring than I had expected. Of course I climbed to the top, whence, from the gallery above the dome, the idea of what the city is, or was intended to be, reveals itself. The Washington Monument, designed to be 600 feet high, is perhaps the most striking sign of incomplete-

INTERIOR OF THE HOUSE OF REPRESENTATIVES.

ness seen from the Capitol, for it has stopped short at 170 feet, and looks like what it is, the stump of a column. I went into the House of Representatives and the Senate, which flank the Capitol, and are approached by doors and passages from the rotunda under the dome. They are oblong chambers, the House of Representatives being 139 feet by 93, and a little larger than the other; but they both look very low, since they are only 30 feet high. I believe, however, that they suit the voice. The seats are spread out like a fan from the Speaker's chair. Reporters are excellently placed, and galleries afford seats to some 1,200 persons. This may sometimes be a questionable convenience, as the directness of debate is likely to be affected by the presence of a crowd, none of whom need "members' orders" for admission to the House. ' The ceilings are panelled and decorated, and desks are provided for members.

The Patent Office is an immense building. Americans are inventive, and here a model is shown of every patent taken out and rejected. These last are placed together. Somehow I had omitted noticing this fact in the guide book I consulted, and where I saw it stated after I had left the place. The models are made to scale, but as they are all small, the collection has rather a toyish appearance. Any visitor can have a model he wishes to examine brought out for him. Intending patentees, therefore, may look through the class of models to which their projected invention belongs, and calculate the chances of its novelty. Great facilities are afforded to inventors, and an American patent is, I believe, altogether the cheapest and most secure in the world. The clerks and attendants are ready in giving all information needed. No fees are asked or expected from visitors to this or any other public building in Washington. No soldiers mount guard anywhere. All Departments are open to the public from 10 A.M. to 3 P.M., a permit from the Secretary of the Treasury being needed only for the inspection of the printing of "greenbacks."

The Treasury is another huge, roomy place, about 500 feet long and a little under 300 broad. I was too late when I visited this, but saw the White House. I did not, indeed, intend to seek admission into it, for the President was at home, and I thought it might be closed. However, I walked up to look at the outside. It deserves the name of the White House, even in a city of white edifices, for everything about it—the glaring road, the blinds, the door itself—helped to claim the title. I saw no one about, no sentries, no servants of any kind. A soldier's horse was tied up at the entrance, but everything stood quiet and still in the bright sunshine. Presently four persons, Americans, whom I had seen doing the sights of Washington, and whom, indeed, I had not long before directed to the spiral staircase which leads up the dome of the Capitol, came saunter- ing out. They walked away, and the door was shut behind them. Another orderly rode up, tied his horse to a ring in the portico, and walked in. I turned aside, and was strolling off, supposing the White House was closed to visitors for the day, when an old negress came smiling out by some side door.

" Mornin', sar," said she. " Mornin', marm," said I. I supposed her to be a sort of Aunt Sally among the servants, and asked her if the house was still open. " Bless, you, sar," she replied, " I've been there three hours ; but I didn't see the President after all." " Did you want to see him ?" " Yes, sar ; wages very low, work scarce." " Did you expect him to find you any ?" " Well, sar, I thought I'd go and see, but he is busy." Then she volunteered her opinion on his fitness for his post, and praised Lincoln. " Ah ! I do believe he was a Christian."

Negroes are monstrously communicative. Unlike Americans, they frequently begin the conversation, and are generally very ambitious in their choice of subjects. The negro's talk is as large as his lips. He is always contemplating a long journey, or deliver- ing himself about the greatest matters and the biggest people. The black barber talks of setting up business in London. The boots at the hotel discusses the relation between Canada and the United States. A man who sold pears to us in the train to Richmond mixed up his opinion of Henry Clay, *à propos* to nothing, with his offers of fruit. This negress laid down the law about the qualification of the Chief Magistrate with most entertaining decision, and was quite sincere in intending to place her special necessities before none less than the President himself. There was a grotesque pathos in the faith she felt in her appeal to the head of the Government.

But he was busy. Busy! I should think so, if he has to listen to every personal tale. However, Aunt Sally provoked me at least to look into the house, so I retraced my steps and rang the front bell. A servant out of livery opened the door at once, and began showing me over the place. I said I was an Englishman passing through Washington, and hoped I was not too late to see the White House. "O no, sir," he replied, "but you must not expect to see such a palace as you have in England." While we were looking about I said, "I suppose the President is much pressed upon by visitors." "Well," he rejoined, "there are pretty many, but I am sure he would see you if you walked up-stairs." "I won't trouble him," said I; "besides, I have not come prepared to seek a presentation." I referred to my dress—wideawake and overcoat, which I wore because the wind was

keen, though the sun was bright. He saw what I
meant and laughed, adding, "We don't think about
that ,here, sir." So I strolled up the stairs, which
were public, and found myself, without introduction,
in a large room, where General —— was hearing an
application from some contractor at a table, a secretary
sitting at another, and an old gentleman standing
before the fire with an unlit cigar in his mouth. A
negro porter sat by a door on the other side of the
room.

The General, too, asked me most courteously if I
wanted to see the President. I replied that had I
known he received that day I would have sought,
with others, the honour of making my bow to him,
but that I did not like to go in as I was. He smiled,
and said that made no difference, and added, " Send
your card in. Sit down." So I gave him my card
and sat down, while he went on with his business.
In a minute or two I was called into an inner room,
and found the President standing before the fire
smoking a cigar. He was exceedingly courteous, and
honoured me with some conversation about Utah and
the great line, the former of which he knew much
about personally, having been there. Then I made
my bow, he shook hands, and I went out certainly
much impressed with the extreme facility of access
granted by the head of the Government to visitors.
The whole thing was so unexpectedly informal that I

THE WHITE HOUSE.

felt it difficult to realise that I had had an interview with so great a personage as the President of the United States. He is a very gentlemanly man, with a quiet, deliberate voice, and an eye that looks straight at you when he speaks. He wore an ordinary morning dress, almost scrupulously well-fitting; and I noticed that, like the majority of Americans, he had a small white hand and very neat boots.

There can be no greater mistake than to represent the conventional American in a tail coat and bulgy boots. I did not notice a tail coat worn in the morning while in America, nor did I ever see a more clean heeled race in my life. Even in the rough West, where trousers are worn stuffed into " Wellingtons " —though they are not known by that name there— the boots were almost invariably neatly built. Our guide in the Sierra wore a high-heeled pair, which might have come out of the most fashionable shop in Regent Street.

The President is exposed to much detail of work, which must be very wearisome. He receives, I forget whether it is twice or three times a week, and is, of course, constantly pestered with personal applications for office. It was exceedingly good-natured in him to see me, a wandering Englishman, as he did after the reception hours had passed. No one, moreover, could be more pleasantly courteous than General ——, with whom, before I left, I had some very agreeable conversation. And this courtesy descends to lower officials. Again and again I ventured to introduce myself to such as the officers of Public Charity and Correction, and Emigration, and nowhere did I find a " Jack in office." All everywhere offered me all the facilities in their power, often putting themselves to trouble in showing me what I wanted to see. The ordinary attendants, moreover, never seemed to expect a fee. Only once did I have a hint of the kind, and that was from a convict boat crew, in party-coloured dresses, when their officer offered to row me across the East River from the Penitentiary. They suggested that they had no " baccy."

The absence of formality in American institutions is very striking. Perhaps it is most so in the law courts. We find it difficult to realise a judge on the bench in a frock coat and pointed moustache. And as the prisoner stands on the floor of the court, which is covered with chairs, in which the counsel sit in all manner of beards and easy morning dress, it is somewhat difficult at first to realise who is who and what is going on. The friends of the prisoner sit below, close by the counsel, in a place reserved for them.

But I must close this rambling chapter. I left Washington impressed with a mingled sense of magnificence, incompleteness, and simplicity. No place has a finer Capitol, no nation has a more accessible chief magistrate, and I should think no city is as yet so imperfectly realised as the metropolis of the United States of America.

PRESIDENT GRANT.

CHAPTER XV.

RELIGION IN THE UNITED STATES.

I SIT down to devote a chapter to the aspect of religion in the United States, specially in reference to the Episcopal Church; and I do so with some hesitation, for though I have seen and heard a good deal of the working of that church, I cannot allow my pen to run so freely on these matters as I have on such outside phases of daily life as present themselves to the ordinary tourist in America. Let me, however, set down some of the impressions I have received.

I was not prepared to find such strong evidences of popular respect for religion as met me everywhere during my tour. I found them not only in the city and the country, but in the forest, the steamboat, and the railway station. While in the Yo Semite Valley I was at once asked to hold a service on Sunday. The Californian steamboat had a notice full of godly advice to young men posted in the saloon; and, to give a characteristic instance of the importunity with which religion occasionally presents itself in the

United States, let me tell you that when I bought a
sleeping-car ticket at Sacramento for my long journey
eastward across the Continent, the clerk, on learning
I was a clergyman, took me to task for travelling by
a train in which I should have to spend the Sunday.
Of course I did not choose Sunday travelling, but in
these long journeys it is sometimes very difficult to
avoid it; and when once I tried to do so, starting on
a Monday morning, I did not get away from the train
till the following Sunday night. However, on the
occasion to which I refer, the clerk, knowing the
length of the journey, and not knowing or asking
what my engagements were, took upon himself to
rebuke me for securing a sleeping berth when I did.
The man was perfectly sincere, and I mention the
matter to show how religious feeling rises to the
surface in America. This was far from being a
solitary instance of similar punctiliousness. Indeed,
a clergyman using the simple natural freedom of an
English Christian must expect to find Americans
sometimes provokingly exacting when he travels in
their country. Again and again I came across phases
of religious severity which were strikingly importunate,
if not always radically matured. There is a sort of
tartness, like that of unripe fruit, in some growths of
American religion. The old Puritan stock still bears
strong crops, and spiritual food is frequently given
before it has time to mellow. Americans are very

fond of rules and regulations, and this taste shows itself often in the conventional codes of piety which are adopted by the various Churches. In their country private judgment is more or less limited to the choice of some particular community, the members of which profess the same opinions and look sharply after each other. I am bound to say, however, that one Church will receive members from another; but the names of applicants are submitted to the congregation with whom they wish to be in communion. I have heard them read out on Sunday. All this shows the prevalence of a minute ecclesiastical supervision which runs through the whole mass of professing Christians in America. I except, of course, the Romish Church, which holds no communion with others; and I have reason to believe that the "Protestant Episcopal," or, as it is more generally called, the "Episcopal," takes a more exclusive attitude than other Protestant communities. All, however, are called ."Churches." The term "Dissenter" or "Nonconformist" is, of course, unknown; and a "chapel" is merely the building attached to a church for the purpose of meetings, lectures, subsidiary services, Sunday-schools, &c. There is no body corresponding to a national church which admits catholicity of views among its members. Churches and parties are sharply defined, though, as I have said, among the chief Protestant communities there

is some interchange of membership, and ministers
frequently unite in the prosecution of some common
object.   But the views of the majority prevail in each
church.   A congregation of Episcopalians is, I think,
throughout the country, more distinctly high or low
than with us.   I say "congregation," because the
word "parish," as understood in England, has no
meaning in America.   It is constantly used, but in a
congregational, not territorial, sense.   And there
seems to be no real representation of the minority
in the government of any church.   The minority
must conform or depart.   There is practically no
historical code or supreme court to which appeal may
be made by such as cannot trim their sentiments to
any which may possess the current or prevailing
majority.   A margin of a few High or Low Church-
men among the Episcopalians can by their votes
colour the whole government of the church, and
procure the promotion of the adherents of their own
party alone.   One effect, however, of the American
system is to promote schism.   A party gets pre-
eminence and keeps the other out of place.   And this
is a process which accumulates in intensity till the
baffled minority breaks off and forms a new community for itself.   When that is done, there may be
an interchange of some offices between the two bodies,
but till then the member of a church who cannot
always think according to order is in a somewhat

depressed and irritating position. I have, for instance, been struck with the paucity, if not absence, of those whom we call "Broad" in the American Episcopal Church. I was almost going to say that they were "nowhere" in that body. And from what I could make out, this applies in some measure to all American religious communities. A man belongs to some party, and that party has a representative "church" which holds some friendly relations with others, but expects its own members to think in unison far more than the members of the Church of England do. There is more choice of opinions than individual liberty of judgment.

The result of this is a conglomeration of sects which forms the nearest approach to a national Church. Among these there is in the main some informal good understanding, but no one would care to claim or allow anything like authoritative pre-eminence, except, of course, the Romish Church, which recognises nothing but itself. Each governs itself; there is no fixed common representative accredited body. Some may unite for a passing purpose, but such union is only temporary. The American Church, in the largest sense, is a congeries of religious republics which have no permanent federation.

Each being, however, as it were, a republic, wide religious provision is made for the masses of the people. There is little in America corresponding to

the provision of the means of Divine worship for the
" poor " of which we hear in England.   I have heard
this brought as a charge against American Churches.
But the real answer, to speak generally, is that there
are few "poor," as we understand the word.   Large
numbers of the working classes who might be loosely
classed as " poor " with us are, as far as my obser-
vation has gone—and I have attended many services,
or looked in while they were being held—in the habit
of attending some place of worship.   I have seen
congregations of Methodists or Baptists where any one
with an eye for the social position of the material of a
crowd could perceive at once that those present did
not belong to what we, perhaps, would call the upper
or middle classes.

Moreover, we are too ready to form an opinion on
the general religious provision for the " masses " in
America from what we see in cities.   The sub-division
of the land into small parcels, each worked by the
owner of the soil, his family, and some " farmers,"
as agricultural labourers are called in America (these
last sometimes living in the land-owner's house),
provides a class which to a great extent occupies the
place and does the work of such as are commonly
known as poor in England.   Thus the bulk of the
real American people are found in the country.   The
city poor are mainly Irish Roman Catholics, who are
looked after by their own priests with much external

success, if I may judge by the character of the congregations I have seen in Roman Catholic churches. Hence the religious provision for many who look poor in the streets of a city is accounted for. Then there are the negroes, who are chiefly Baptists, and have their own places of worship. Then consider, as I have said, how the real masses of Americans are spread over the country. Look at the little wooden church in every village. See how the spire or tower, staring with paint and æsthetically ugly as possible, shows itself in a new settlement, and ask, " Who build these—who attend them ? " The real " working men " of America.

The people have reversed the process with which we are familiar in England. Instead of having money begged for them by others for a church, they build it themselves; and instead of having a parson set amongst them, they look about and " call " some one to be their minister. It is the same in education. Here the parson begs and scrapes to get a school built—there he looks out of his window and sees the thing done without his moving a finger.

No doubt there are outlying or isolated settlements, or half nomadic gatherings of miners, where difficulty is felt in making provision for public worship and pastoral ministrations. The Episcopal Church is exerting itself much to meet cases of this kind, especially in the mining districts of the West. But the bulk of the people look after themselves, and churches in the main are self-feeding. We have one very exceptional case in the Church Mission in the Salt Lake City. There the great want is a house of refuge, as it might be called, for those—many of them once poor members of the Church of England—who are growing weary of their perversion to Mormonism. They can hardly form a community strong and rich enough to build a church. They are specially hampered, and it is hoped that some help may be sent from the old country, whence a large proportion of Mormons have been recruited.

The American clergy work at high pressure. They have—I speak now of the Episcopal—to keep an account of all the services they have held, sermons they have preached, lectures they have delivered, &c., &c., which, with the numbers of those baptized, confirmed, and admitted to the Holy Communion, is printed, and public property. This is likely, in some cases, to induce an unwholesome air of competition, and several times I heard remarks made upon the report of such and such a clergyman as not exhibiting a genuine test of the work accomplished. But whatever a man does or leaves undone is exposed to lay and clerical scrutiny. Every minister of religion lives and works in the full glare of the public eye, and runs his course with the spur of public opinion in his side.

I confess that I did not like divers of the services in the Episcopal church which I attended. Any of our brethren in America who may read this must forgive me when I say, that I was sometimes struck to the backbone by their coldness. Respectability seemed to rein supreme. That is, however, an essential feature in American religious gatherings. In church there was frequently but little responding. The choir, consisting generally of ladies and gentlemen in a gallery, as a rule sings to the congregation, which listens. Some of the clergy feel this painfully. At one church where I assisted in the service, on being asked some question afterwards in the vestry, I could not help saying that I thought the Te Deum rather long. It was very elaborately sung, one young lady taking a prominent solo part. "Te Deum!" said the Rector; "it is what I call Tedious.' The failure in congregational music is more striking in some Episcopal churches, from the habit which some of the congregations have of sitting while the hymns are sung to them. The best congregational singing I heard in America was in Mr. Ward Beecher's church in Brooklyn. The next to that was in an Episcopal church at the corner of Sixth Avenue and Twentieth Street, in New York. This church is, I believe, almost unique in its way. The seats are all free and unappropriated. There is not much of what is called ritual, since the choir of men and boys who chant

antiphonally in choir seats at the east end are not
even surpliced.

One thing which struck me in almost all the congregations I saw was the large, in some instances
very large, proportion of men present. The defect in
responding does not, I believe, arise from indifference
to the service, but rather from the silence, which is a
striking feature of American gatherings. Religion
there is an eminently pressing—nay, sometimes importunate—matter of general public concern, and men
do not leave its observances to be attended by what
have been called " bonnets and babies." The man
element is very conspicuous. I went to the St.
Alban's—so named—of New York, where the service
is highly ritualistic, candles being lighted on the
altar during celebration, banners carried, wafer bread
used, &c. Here the seats are free and unappropriated; but as there were, at least where I myself
worshipped, no kneeling-boards or hassocks, many sat
during prayers. The church is small, there being
possibly room to seat 300. It struck me that the
proportion of women was greater here than elsewhere.
I am inclined to suspect that " ritualism " will not
commend itself much to Americans; but whatever
, else may be thought about it, the service at St.
Alban's in New York is a bold attempt to break
through the cold crust of public worship in the States.
I should say that one of the warmest services I

attended in America was in the cathedral at Chicago, which has a surpliced choir, without what we understand by ritualism. There was a fine congregation, and, especially in the evening, a hearty congregational service. As far as I could understand it, however, generally the style of service in the Episcopal Church was what is sometimes called "high and dry" with us. Again I remark, that the coldness I noticed must be attributed more to what appeared to me a national spirit of silence, if not sadness, than to indifference. Americans struck me as naturally pre-occupied and reserved, and their reserve shows itself when they are particularly serious. I shall not easily forget the impression I received in one Presbyterian church. I went in while the singing was going on, and anything more dismal I have seldom seen or heard.

Almost all the churches I saw were extremely comfortable. The seats, and in some cases the backs, were softly cushioned. The best sermons, at least those which appeared heartiest, were in Presbyterian and Congregationalist places of worship. But what I think surprised me most was the "orthodoxy" of sentiments I heard in a Unitarian and Universalist church. In the latter, where there was a magnificent congregation with a large proportion of men, the minister laid down the doctrine of the Atonement with extreme minuteness of detail. In another, a non-Episcopalian church—I really cannot say to what denomination it belonged—I heard, I think, the driest, boniest sermon I ever listened to, and that is saying much. The preacher was discoursing on the verse in the sixth chapter of St. John—"Except ye eat the flesh of the Son of Man," &c. He said: "This cannot be understood literally, for such a supposition would offend the best feelings of propriety." The congregation looked as if especially accessible to such an appeal. The most magniloquent sermon I heard was by a black minister in a negro Baptist church.

Episcopalians have the character of presenting the most "respectable" congregations. I cannot say that I perceived this. A large proportion of the most educated classes are, however, said to belong to the Episcopal Church. It is decidedly influential, but comes low in the list, if we may judge by the number of its adherents. Methodist, Baptist, Congregationalist, and Presbyterian Churches are much more numerous, the two former at least counting five or six among their followers where the Episcopal Church counts one. The latter, however, is generally admitted to be growing; and it has lately exhibited a fresh movement in the support of home missionary work, and it numbers notoriously some most devoted men among its bishops and ministers.

I must be allowed to state that the clergy in America would not generally be considered by Eng-

INTERIOR OF CATHEDRAL CHURCH, CHICAGO (FROM A PHOTOGRAPH).

lishmen as clerical in their appearance. I have seen the rector of an eminent Episcopal church wear a black neckcloth while officiating on Sunday. This applies also to ministers of other denominations. It is frequently very difficult to distinguish a clergyman by his dress. My impression for some time was that no clergymen were to be met in the streets.

It struck me that clergymen are treated with great respect in America. I have, unasked, had an abatement made in the price of an article because I was a clergyman. Some railways carry ministers free, and I was told it was not an unusual thing for a company to present a bishop with a free pass over all its lines. Indeed, I was advised myself always to mention my cloth in taking a ticket, as 25 per cent. would be deducted from its price. I did not do this, and so cannot vouch from experience for the effect of the statement.

From lay and clerical sources I gathered that the clergy, as a rule, are far from being ill-paid in the United States. In some cases congregations even meet the expenses of a tour when their minister is in need of exceptional rest, and provide funds for a sub-stitute while he is away. Americans do not grudge their clergy liberal stipends when they like them, but an unpopular man feels his unpopularity in a material sense.

I cannot conclude this chapter without saying that

nothing could surpass the kindness of those Episcopal clergy I met. With no exception they all spoke in the handsomest and friendliest manner of the Church of England; and, as far as I was personally concerned, I can never thank them enough for the cordiality with which they held out their hands to a mere stranger like myself.

CHAPTER XVI.

SOME ACCOUNT OF THE LANDING AND TREATMENT OF EMIGRANTS IN NEW YORK.

As popular interest in emigration is increasing, perhaps our readers may like an account of the reception and treatment of emigrants at New York. I assisted in the landing and disposal of some 1,200.

They set foot first in America on the tip of the tongue of land on which New York is situated. A large heavy circular building stands there. It was once a fort, but is now called " Castle Gardens," and is the receiving-house of the Emigration Commissioners. It will shelter many hundred emigrants. Outside it, towards the bay, is a wooden landing-stage. The emigrant ships lie some distance off, and send their loads on shore in steam-tenders.

Having, on a comparatively blank day at Castle Gardens, presented an introduction to the general agent, Mr. Casserly, he kindly put me into the hands of a gentleman, who took me round and showed me to all the officers, as one with the privilege of entry. This was needful, as otherwise I was liable to be

BROADWAY, NEW YORK (FROM A PHOTOGRAPH).

summarily turned out if found on the premises while
emigrants were being landed, or I should have had no
time to exhibit a pass and justify my presence all
about the place during the bustle of a reception-day.
I was shown the landing-stage, the passage from it
into the Rotunda, the desks at which the clerks sat
to greet the new-comers, the various counters at which
different kinds of information were given, the waiting-
room of friends, the refreshment place, and Labour
Exchange. The whole process of the reception of
emigrants was then explained to me, that I might
know what to look for and what to do when I
came.

Next morning I went down to see the establishment at work. I found it quite empty of all but the
officials, who were at their posts with books open,
ready to begin. Two large ships, full of emigrants,
were lying in the bay about three-quarters of a mile
off. The tender was alongside one of them, taking
in her load. I walked to the bare landing-stage and
waited. The tender soon left the ship, her deck being
apparently heaped with people like currants on a tray.
She came slowly up towards the quay, and presently
I perceived a bank of white faces, all turned one way,
and a thousand eyes all straining at the shore. As
she bumped gently against the stage, and a railed
plank was run out to her deck, there was a sway and
rush among the emigrants to get on land. " Gently

there !" cried the officer in command; " one at a time, please." After I had seen the stream begin to pour out, I ran back into the building, and took my place behind a counter by a clerk whose business it was to put down the names. The passage to this admitted the people in single file. The first face soon came, looking very bewildered. " Name, please," said the clerk kindly. " Bridget Nolan, sir." " Where do you come from, Bridget ?" and his cheery voice calmed her face down at once. " Mayo, sir." " Ever been here before, Bridget ?" " No, sir." " Where are you going, eh ?" " Illinois." Thus he inquired all about her, and putting the particulars down as quick as lightning, pointed to where she should wait. The string of emigrants hearing all this, and seeing how the thing was managed so far, came up primed with their answers. There were men and women of all ages, some quite old. Presently there appeared two tiny heads hardly reaching to the counter. They were those of a little boy and girl about eight and nine years of age. She was the eldest, and held her brother's hand in her left, while she clutched tightly in her right the brass check which had been given them for their one small piece of luggage.

" Anybody with these children ?" said the clerk. " No, sir," replied a woman, who had six of her own crowding close behind her; " but they have been along with mine in the ship, and I have done what I could by them." "How old are you, my dears?" asked the clerk, leaning over towards them. They shook their heads; they didn't know. "Come in here," said he. Then I brought the two trots inside the counter, and set them down by the fire. They held one another very tight. On asking if they were hungry, they nodded; both of them. So I got them a good hunch of bread and meat from the refreshment place, and went back to my post by the clerk, while they fell to at once, in silence.

The putting down of the names was soon over. Practice does wonders in this business. Thus all were registered, and waited in the wide space in the Rotunda, outside the counter. Then those who had money to buy railway tickets had them supplied. After this, a clerk got into a sort of pulpit, and desiring the attention of the emigrants, told them that he was going to call out the names of those who had letters or money orders waiting for them. As they answered, these were put into their hands. Then he called out the names of those who had friends in another room, where they were taken, as they answered, by an official. These processes were repeated, lest any at the first roll-call should have missed their names.

At last the crowd was sifted down to those who had no money of their own, no letters, and no friends.

More about these presently. Those who had paid for their tickets were packed off the same day to their destination in the country. Those who wanted to stay in New York, and could pay for their maintenance, were introduced to special respectable lodging-house keepers, licensed by the Mayor, and carried off by them. Those who had friends in the waiting-room were let go on being claimed, but not without, in several instances, careful examination of both parties by an officer as to whether the claim was true. This part of the business was very touching. I went with the introducing official. Generally the recognition was obviously genuine. Eyes met, and people rushed together. The woman with the six children, who had been kind to the two babes on the voyage, pounced on me in the Rotunda, eagerly asking, "Where is my husband? I know he must be somewhere about; I saw him rowing round the ship in a little boat: I thought he would be here." "All right, mother," said I, "he is in the next room;" and I took her in. She was far too grateful to think of thanking me. There he was, and a cheery, broad-shouldered fellow he was, too. How they all blocked up the passage with their family embrace! They made quite a little mob. How he kissed her and hugged the children all round! How they leaped upon him! "Come now," said the officer, good-humouredly, "you really must let these other people get at their friends." So they trooped out, all flustered with joy.

Some who had no particular destination, but intended simply to seek work in America, went at once, free of charge, into the Labour Exchange, a large office in Castle Gardens, where employers or their agents were waiting to engage labour. Clerks sat behind counters, over which were written up the names of the various trades in which work was then to be found. The wages being given that day were —Labourers, 1 dollar 75 cents to 2 dollars a day; tailors, up to 20 dollars a week; carpenters, 25 dollars a month and board, or 18 dollars a week without beard; bricklayers, 5 dollars a day; farmers, *i.e.*, agricultural labourers, 12 to 14 dollars a month and board; shoemakers, 6 to 15 dollars a week. These were the figures I took down from the clerks. " Farmers" get more in the summer, sometimes as much as 25 or 30 dollars a month with board, in the West. Tailors and shoemakers, whose *maximum* wages were 20 and 15 dollars, received in many cases much less, the claims of some to work at their respective trades being almost nominal.

So much for the Labour Exchange, which seemed to be conducted with much care and to do a great deal of business. Some of the newly landed emigrants found work at once through this institution, a record being kept of the various engagements entered into by its means, thus affording the Commissioners of Emigration an easy method of reference in case of complaint, and the emigrants a convenient mode of tracing friends who had gone before them.

The baggage of those thus engaged, as well as of those who were sent off by rail or otherwise disposed of, having been examined on board ship, was given to them afterwards. They had checks for it, being allowed to bring none but hand-parcels into the Rotunda. I should add, that, beside provision of railway tickets, there were counters for general information, assistance in letter-writing, telegraphic messages, and exchange of money. Clerks in attendance spoke and wrote the various Continental languages.

Let us now go back to those without money, letters, or friends. They formed a dismal party, and had to shake down that night as well as they could, under supervision, in the Rotunda. Next day they were put on board a steamer and sent to Ward's Island, about an hour off, up the river. I went with them. Divers were in tears. One woman in particular was loud in her sorrow. She had expected to find her husband, and found neither him nor any message. She had four or five small children with her. The officers told me that the friends of emigrants in America often waited till they saw in the papers the arrival of the ship in which their relations were to come, and, knowing that they would be cared for by the Emigration

Commissioners, did not write or make their appearance for a day or two. Thus I was glad to learn that the two lone children would be accounted for. They had a father in the States, who had caused them to be shipped for America, like parcels, to be kept till called for. But this woman would not be comforted. As she was embracing her children, and lamenting in the broadest Devonshire accent, I said to her, "Don't be frightened, my good friend; from what part of Devonshire do you come?" This touched the vein of her sorrow. She turned to me as to a deliverer, and dried her tears when she found that I knew something of her home. I explained all about the place she was going to, the strong probability of her being soon fetched away by her husband, and cheered her wonderfully.

Among the emigrants was an Irishman, shrewd enough in some things, but rather bewildered at what was being done with him. He thought he was going to some workhouse. He told me where he came from, and said that he had expected letters. I made him more comfortable in mind, and gave him some tobacco. "Now," said I, "tell me all about it." I give his story, translated from the strongest brogue, but very touchingly narrated by him.

"Sir," he said, "I have had two brothers in America for some years. I thought I would stay behind, as I had fourteen acres of land, and thought it would go hard if I could not get my living out of it. So I dug and drained, and all promised well. Then, one day, the agent came to me, and, says he, 'I can get double the rent for that land now, Mike, and you must pay it or go.' So I went. But I have given all that work to the landlord for nothing. I assure you, sir," he continued, "I know violence is wrong, but when these things are done, a man's mind is upset; he forgets himself."

Then he paused for a moment, spat into the river, and added, " Sir, I've known 'em lie behind a hedge with a revolver—men like me. I know it's wrong. I said to myself, 'I'll go. I'll leave this place and go to the Land of God.' So I am here, though I have only feasted my eyes upon the shore, and not set foot upon it yet." It was a hard case.

Along with the other passengers were some dregs of emigration: tattered, greasy, blear-eyed. The Commissioners bind themselves to provide shelter in the State of New York to emigrants for some time after they land, in case they are in tribulation. And some prefer chronic tribulation. They earn a little money, drink, are turned off, and throw themselves upon the Commissioners. There were two or three of these poor rascals on board. Besides them were sick emigrants going to the hospital on Ward's Island. Presently we landed, and all trooped up to the receiving office. There I presented my introduction, and was

asked to take a seat by the chief behind his counter.
The party was soon disposed of.   Some were sent to
the refuge, where they had work to do, but were fed
and lodged.   Some were dismissed to the hospital.
The children were sent to school, but not separated
from their parents.   Then came the turn of the most
prominent rascal.   The officer glanced up.   " Drunk
again, I suppose."   " Yes, sir," said the man, sheep-
ishly.   " Go into that corner," replied the officer.
They make the place uncomfortable to these gentry,
though the Commissioners are obliged to feed them.

When the crowd was melted down, the officer took
me over the establishment.   It appeared to me to be
well managed.   The Commissioners hold more than
one-half of the island, or about 121 acres.   The buildings are the refuge, and the hospital proper, reserved
exclusively for non-contagious diseases and surgical
cases ; there are also fever hospitals—placed near the
water and isolated,—the lunatic asylum, dispensary,
barracks, nursery, surgical wards, and residences for
the officers.   There are two chapels, one Episcopal, and
one Roman Catholic, each holding about 500.   Representatives of religious bodies and societies may distri-
bute religious books and papers among the emigrants,
and may report to the officers any wants not of a
religious nature.   They may also visit any sick in the
hospital as often as their presence is desired by
patients.

The lunatic asylum was especially distressing. The poor sufferers appeared to be treated with much kindness, but the proportion of lunatics is great. I was told that some who had built their hopes on emigration, and come out with vague ideas of meeting friends at once, had gone mad, on finding their hopes suddenly dashed to the ground.

Attached to the refuge is a farm, on which many emigrants are set to work till they can get employment. In the previous year, the total number of inmates cared for and treated in all the various establishments, including hospitals and refuge, was 14,250; the total number dead, or discharged in the same period being 12,249. Thus 2,001 were left in December, 1868. These destitute, sick, or temporarily friendless, form a small proportion of the emigrants received and disposed of by the Commissioneers in the twelve months. The total number landed was, in 1868, 213,686.

I will not weary our readers with statistics, which I take out of the published report of the Commissioners to the Legislature of the State of New York, but I might mention that there was in 1868 a decrease in alien emigration of 29,045 from the number received in 1867; but an increase over the average of the previous twenty years, of 22,421. Germans came in proportionately larger numbers. These amounted to 101,989; Irish to 47,571; English to 29,695; and all other countries together to 34,431; showing a decrease of 37,182 in the emigration from Germany, Ireland, and England together, but an increase of 8,137 in the miscellaneous emigration. The most marked feature in this latter item is the great number of emigrants from Sweden. Among the year's arrivals were 7,390 Scotch, 2,811 French, 699 Welsh, 268 Poles, 149 Belgians, 33 Australians, 22 Turks, 10 Africans, 3 Japanese, and 1 Sardinian.

The advantages held out to emigrants by the Commissioners are very great. The chief one is care for some time after landing, in case they become sick or fail in getting employment, either in Ward's Island or in places throughout the State of New York where such help is needed. The Commissioners keep an account with country agents and institutions, to whom the needy emigrants apply.

The revenues of the institution arises from the payment by ship-owners to the Commissioners of about five shillings a head. This is virtually paid by the emigrants, being included in their passage-money.

The result is that the Commissioners have some control over ship-owners, and can care for the comfort of emigrants on board ship. By an Act of the Legislature of the State of New York passed in 1867, the Commissioners are generally invested with the power (subject to certain conditions) of examining under oath any witness respecting complaints; and such testimony, if made in the presence of the persons complained of, may be used as evidence in any subsequent action between any of the passengers and the owners, masters, or charterers of the ship.

The financial position of this great institution is good. The Commissioners had, on January 1, 1868, a balance of 6,865,013 dollars.

There are many interesting details in the "Report of the Commissioners of Emigration of the State of New York." I have tried to give a general idea of their work and position, which is not so well known as it should be.

I must add that nothing could exceed the courtesy with which I was treated by all the officials.

THE END.

LONDON:
PRINTED BY JAS. TRUSCOTT AND SON,
Suffolk Lane, City.

PUBLICATIONS

OF THE

Society for Promoting Christian Knowledge.

Most of these works may be had in ornamental bindings, with gilt edges, at a small extra charge.

	Price.
	s. *d.*

ADELBERT AND BASTEL. A Story for Children. Translated from the German by permission of the Author. 18mo. cloth boards 1 0

A JOURNAL OF THE PLAGUE YEAR. Being Observations, or Memorials, of the most Remarkable Occurrences, as well Public as Private, which happened in London during the last great Visitation in 1665. Written by a Citizen who continued all the while in London. Imp. 16mo. cloth boards ... 3 0

A STEADFAST WOMAN. By the Author of "Eric Thorburn" and "Cecy's Recollections." Reprinted from "The People's Magazine." Demy 8vo. cloth boards 3 0

ALONE AMONG THE ZULUS. By a Plain Woman. The Narrative of a Journey through the Zulu Country, South Africa. Fcp. 8vo. bevelled boards, gilt edges 2 6

BATTLE WORTH FIGHTING, THE; and other Stories. Fcp. 8vo. cloth boards 2 0

CARPENTER'S FAMILY, THE; a Sketch of Village Life. By Mrs. JOSEPH LAMB (RUTH BUCK). With four full-page engravings on toned paper. Crown 8vo. cloth boards 1 6

CHARLEY ASHLEY. The Adventures of an Orphan Boy. With six full-page illustrations on toned paper. By J. G. WALKER, Esq. Crown 8vo. cloth boards 1 6

CHOTA NAGPORE MISSION TO THE KOLS, THE. By the Rev. J. CAVE-BROWNE, M.A., Indian Chaplain in the Diocese of Calcutta. Fcp. 8vo., with map, cloth boards...... 1 6

CHRISTIAN FATHERS, THE. Lives of Ignatius, Polycarp, Justin, Irenæus, Cyprian, Athanasius, Hilary, Basil, Gregory Nazïenzen, Ambrose, Jerome, Chrysostom, Augustine, Gregory the Great, Bede, and Bernard. By the Rev. G. G. PERRY, M.A. Post 8vo. cloth boards 3 6

[Crown 8vo.]

Price.
s. d.

CHURCH OF ENGLAND BIOGRAPHIES. Hooker—Ussher—Herbert—Leighton—Lady Falkland—Jeremy Taylor—Ken—Margaret Godolphin—John Newton. Crown 8vo., with four Portraits, cloth boards 2 0

CHURCH OF ENGLAND BIOGRAPHIES. Second Series. Wilson—Hannah More—Joshua Watson—Legh Richmond—Heber—Blomfield—Dr. Scoresby—Longley—Mackenzie. Crown 8vo., with two Portraits, cloth boards.................. 2 0

CLEAR SHINING AFTER RAIN. (For Girls.) By Mrs. CAREY BROCK. Crown 8vo. cloth boards 3 0

CROYLAND ABBEY: An Historical Sketch. By the Rev. GEORGE G. PERRY. Fcp. 8vo. cloth boards 1 6

CYCLE OF LIFE, THE: a Book of Poems for Young and Old, Town and Country. Printed on toned paper, illustrated with eighteen woodcuts, handsomely bound in cloth, gilt edges, bevelled boards, fcp. 4to. 7 6

DOMINIC. A Story. Translated from the German, by permission of the Author, Franz Hoffman. 18mo. cloth boards 1 0

EARTH'S MANY VOICES. First and Second Series. With illustrations on toned paper. Royal 16mo. extra cloth, gilt edges ....each 2 0

The two series in one volume.................... 4 0

ELLY'S CHOICE, AND WHAT CAME OF IT. 18mo. cloth boards 1 6

FAITHFUL AND TRUE; OR, THE MOTHER'S LEGACY. (For Girls.) Crown 8vo. cloth boards.......................... 1 6

GROSSETESTE, THE LIFE AND TIMES OF ROBERT, BISHOP OF LINCOLN. By the Rev. G. G. PERRY, M.A. Post 8vo. cloth boards.. 2 6

HARRY WATERS AND JOHN HEARD, a Lesson from the Field; or, Like Seed Like Fruit. Crown 8vo. 2 0

HARTZ BOYS, THE; OR, AS A MAN SOWS SO MUST HE REAP. By FRANZ HOFFMAN. Translated from the German. Crown 8vo. cloth boards 1 0

HATTY AND NELLIE; OR, TWO MARRIAGES: a Story of Middle Class Life. By Mrs. CAREY BROCK. Cr. 8vo. cl. bds. 2 6

HELEN FREEMAN'S WORD: a Tale of Field Gang Life. 18mo. cloth boards 1 0

HOME IN SOUTH AFRICA. By the Author of "Alone among the Zulus." Fcp. 8vo. cloth boards...................... 1 6

HOME SUNSHINE; OR, BEAR AND FORBEAR. 18mo. cloth boards 1 0

"IT ISN'T RIGHT;" OR, FRANK JOHNSON'S REASON. By Mrs. JOSEPH LAMB (RUTH BUCK)............................ 1 0

Price.
s. d.

JOHNNY WILKS; OR, THE OLD HOME AND THE NEW. 18mo. cloth boards 1 0

LIFE IN THE WALLS, THE HEARTH, AND THE EAVES. With four full-page illustrations, printed on toned paper, royal 16mo. cloth boards 1 0

LIGHTHOUSE, THE. (For Boys.) 18mo. cloth boards......... 1 0

LIONEL'S REVENGE; OR, THE YOUNG ROYALISTS. Fcp. 8vo. cloth boards 2 0

MARION; OR, THE SMUGGLER'S WIFE. With four full-page illustrations on toned paper, crown 8vo. cloth boards... 2 0

MAYS OF LORTON, THE. A Tale of Village Life. 18mo. cloth boards 1 6

NATURAL HISTORY OF THE BIBLE, THE. By the Rev. H. B. TRISTRAM, M.A., F.L.S. 7 6

NURSE MARGARET'S TWO ST. SYLVESTER EVES. (For Girls.) A Tale. Translated from the German by OTTILIE WILDERMUTH. Royal 16mo. paper boards 0 8

PARABLES OF ANIMALS. By Mrs. BETHAM. With two full-page illustrations on toned paper. Crown 8vo. cloth boards 1 0

POOR LITTLE GASPARD'S DRUM: a Tale of the French Revolution. Fcp. 8vo. cloth boards 1 6

RIGHT WAY AND THE WRONG WAY, THE; OR, THE ARDINGLEY LADS. By A. R. N., author of "Woodbury Farm," "Margaret Vere," &c. With three full-page illustrations on toned paper. Crown 8vo. cloth boards 1 6

RINA CLIFFE. (For Girls.) A Village Character. By E. M. L. With three full-page illustrations on toned paper. Crown 8vo. cloth boards 2 0

RUTH LEE AND HER COMPANIONS; OR, WORKING FOR GOD: a Canadian Story. By the author of the "Two Lucys," &c. 18mo. cloth boards 1 0

SANDWICH ISLANDS AND THEIR PEOPLE, THE. By M. A. DONNE, Author of "Denmark and its People," &c. Fcp. 8vo. cloth boards 2 0

SCENES IN THE EAST. Consisting of Twelve Coloured Photographic Views of Places mentioned in the Bible, beautifully executed. With descriptive Letterpress, by the Rev. H. B. TRISTRAM, M.A., LL.D., F.R.S., &c., author of "The Land of Israel," &c., &c. 4to. cloth, bevelled boards, gilt edges... 7 6

SELBORNE, THE NATURAL HISTORY OF. By the Rev. GILBERT WHITE, A.M., Fellow of Oriel College, Oxford. Arranged for Young Persons. New Edition. Cloth boards. 3 6

Price.
s. d.

SILENT JIM: a Cornish Story. By JAMES F. COBB, Esq., author of "A Tale of Two Brothers." With four full-page illustrations on toned paper. Cloth boards. 3 6

SINAI AND JERUSALEM; OR, SCENES FROM BIBLE LANDS. Consisting of Coloured Photographic Views of Places mentioned in the Bible, including a Panoramic View of Jerusalem. With descriptive Letterpress, by the Rev. F. W. HOLLAND, M.A., Honorary Secretary to the Palestine Exploration Fund. Cloth, bevelled boards, gilt edges......... 7 6

STORIES FOR EVERY SUNDAY IN THE CHRISTIAN YEAR. Fcp. 8vo. cloth boards 2 0

STORIES ON "MY DUTY TOWARDS GOD." Crown 8vo. cloth boards 1 6

STORIES ON "MY DUTIES TOWARDS MY NEIGHBOUR." Crown 8vo. cloth boards 1 6

THE TOPOGRAPHY OF THE HOLY LAND; OR, THE PLACES, RIVERS, AND MOUNTAINS MENTIONED IN THE BIBLE. By the Rev. H. B. TRISTRAM, M.A., LL.D., F.R.S. Crown 8vo. cloth boards 4 0

TO SAN FRANCISCO AND BACK. By a LONDON PARSON. With numerous illustrations. Crown 8vo. cloth boards 2 6

TOM NEAL AND SARAH HIS WIFE, THE EXPERIENCES OF. Crown 8vo. cloth boards 1 6

URSULA'S GIRLHOOD. Fcp. 8vo. cloth boards 1 0

WANDERER, THE. (For Boys.) By Mrs. PEARLESS (late ANNE PRATT). Crown 8vo., with three full-page illustrations, cloth boards 2 0

WINTER IN THE ARCTIC AND SUMMER IN THE ANTARCTIC REGIONS. By C. TOMLINSON. With two Maps. Crown 8vo. cloth boards 4 0

WITHOUT A CHARACTER: a Tale of Servant Life. By Miss POOLE. Crown 8vo. cloth boards 1 0

WRECK OF THE OSPREY, THE: a Story for Boys. Fcp. 8vo. cloth boards 1 6

ZISKA: THE BLIND HERO OF BOHEMIA. A sketch of the Hussite Reformation in the Fifteenth Century. By the Rev. WILLIAM E. HOULDEY. Crown 8vo. cloth boards ... 1 0

Depositories:

77, GREAT QUEEN STREET, LINCOLN'S INN FIELDS;
4, ROYAL EXCHANGE; 48, PICCADILLY;
AND BY ALL BOOKSELLERS.

Lightning Source UK Ltd.
Milton Keynes UK
UKHW020637051218
333474UK00008B/122/P

9 781331 355557